Keep the Pressure up
Aaron!.

Lowell Green

"Once you carry the stain of the English language and culture, no matter where you were born, how long you have lived here, or the number of generations your family has been here, you can never be a full-fledged Quebecois and this can never be your true home. Full membership and participation are denied. You are merely tolerated and you should count yourself lucky at that. After all, you are an undesirable!"

– Kevin Richard, Sherbrooke Record
(One of only two daily English language newspapers left in Quebec).

This book was researched, written, edited, designed, formatted, printed, delivered and sold in Canada by Canadians without any financial assistance from any level of government. In addition, HST in full has been paid at every level of production to editors, publishers, designers, artists, printers, delivery service, accountants, lawyers and advertising. To the best of our knowledge all paper used in this book was manufactured in Canada by Canadian pulp and paper workers.

Spruce Ridge Publishing

ISBN 978-0-9813149-4-5
Printed and bound in Canada
© 2013 Lowell Green

This book was written, published, edited and printed in Canada without the aid of government grants of any nature.

Cover design and book formatting by Tara Yourth/taragraphics.
Cover images - Stock photos: © Kuzma I Dreamstime.com
                                © MorganOliver I Dreamstime.com

Library and Archives Canada Cataloguing in Publication

Green, Lowell, 1936-, author
   Why now is the perfect time to wave a friendly goodbye to Quebec / Lowell Green.

Includes index.
ISBN 978-0-9813149-4-5 (bound)

   1. Sovereignty. 2. Self-determination, National--Québec (Province). 3. Canada--Politics and government--2006-. 4. Québec (Province)--Politics and government--2012-. 5. Québec (Province)--History--Autonomy and independence movements. I. Title.

FC2926.9.S4G74 2013   971.4'05   C2013-905073-6

First Printing September 2013

A shocking change of heart from bestselling author

LOWELL GREEN

WHY NOW

Is The Perfect Time To Wave
A Friendly Goodbye
To Quebec!

Contains the opinions of 90 different Canadians!

This book is dedicated to my wife Deborah.

"Through thick and thin!"

CONTENTS

Foreword 11

That Was Then 15

This Is Now 19

Same Old! Same Old! 23

Would You Take That Trip to Montreal Again? 27

History Tells Us Quebec Separation is Inevitable 45

Independence—It's Bred In The Bone! 49

The Conversion 53

The Shoe Museum 57

Terror Haza 59

Is It Only The Money That keeps Us Together? 63

The Infamous Bill 101 67

Not Wanted! 75

They Got Me! 79

The Exodus Clause 83

The Get Your Business Out of Here Clause 85

The Tongue Troopers 89

A Cynical Assault on Anglo Rights 95

Move Across The River! 99

Driven Out! 103

The Anglophobe Political Complex 109

Where Have All The Angry Anglos Gone? 115

Now Is The Perfect Time To Say Goodbye 121

Of Business Cards And Sin 123

Don't Go West! 125

The People Speak 137

Is It Just English Bigotry? 147

The Great Russell Language War 151

Who Won? 157

The Official Languages Act 159

Hypocrisy In The Workplace 165

Sauce For The Goose Should Be Sauce For The Gander! . . 171

The Cost!!! 177

The Great Fuzzy Dream! 181

A New Kind Of Bilingualism 183

Why Are We Doing It? 189

Only Quebecers Count! 193

The Velvet Divorce! 197

Where Are the Separatists? 203

The Real Question 209

The Great Equalization Con Game 211

Concentrated Stupidity And Cowardice 215

The Native Indian Problem 219

The Voters Say 223

What Happens To Atlantic Canada? 229

We're Bankers To The Separatists! 235

Tomorrow! 239

FOREWORD

In the past six years the Province of Quebec has sucked more than $50 billion in transfer payments from the rest of Canada (ROC). We'll pump close to another $9 billion into the pockets of the separatist (and I believe racist) government this year.

All that "welfare" money while the Province refuses to tap into the 46 billion barrels of oil and trillions of cubic feet of natural gas that have been discovered just beneath the earth's crust along the St. Lawrence. A recent announcement that they would allow some exploratory drilling on Anticosti Island is nothing but a stall tactic.

While Quebec pretends this heel dragging exercise is out of environmental concerns I suspect the real reason is much more devious and totally self-serving. By holding off drilling or fracking for oil and gas until they achieve independence, the separatist government avoids having to share any of the revenue, royalties or taxes with the rest of Canada.

While it is true natural resources are owned by the individual provinces, the federal government exercises control over inter-provincial and international trade and shares jurisdiction of many environmental matters with the provinces. The federal government would also, of course, collect billions in various forms of taxes.

To give you some idea of the kind of money we're talking about, consider this.

The Canadian Energy Research Institute (CERI) estimates that the oil sands of Alberta will create $444 billion in tax revenue across Canada in the next 25 years. More than 70 per cent of that—$322 billion will go the federal government. These figures do not include any revenues or taxes from the sale of natural gas or oil from sources in the province other than the oil sands.

Obviously, as an independent nation, Quebec would not have to fork over a single cent of royalties or taxes to the rest of Canada. They would own and control it all, lock, stock and barrel!

It is doubtful that Quebec would be able to extract oil at a volume comparable to that of Alberta, but no matter which way you look at it, tens of billions of dollars are at stake.

It boils down to this. As part of Canada, any revenue, royalties or taxes from the development of Quebec oil and gas would have to be shared at least in part with the federal government and thus the rest of Canada. In addition, the federal government would be able to exercise considerable control over the industry, in particular many matters relating to environmental concerns as well as inter-provincial and international trade.

But, as an independent nation, Quebec would have full control over the industry and retain the income in all its forms!

Machiavellian? Yes it is. But then what in Quebec these days is not?

At the very least we can stop or slow down the flow of money from the rest of Canada (ROC) into Quebec in 2014 when the Harper Government must renew, amend or cancel the equalization program which very clearly is a flagrant abuse of ROC taxpayers.

Depriving Quebec of its yearly "please stay with us bribe" or greatly reducing it, would probably provide the Province with a final gentle nudge out the Canadian door and force them to follow Alberta's lead, tap into their vast storehouse of oil and gas and become not only self sufficient—but one of the most prosperous countries in the world, perhaps even rivalling Saudi Arabia!

This incredible oil and gas bonanza they thus far refuse to exploit, completely refutes the long held belief that Quebec will never separate because it cannot afford to. As Yogi Berra (or someone) once said, "this really changes the old ball game don't it?"

There's something else that must change as well, because while the assumption has always been that the decision whether to stay or leave will always be that of Quebec, I am suggesting here that the time has come for all of us Canadians to have a say in something this vital.

It could be argued, and I do so here, that separation, no matter whose decision it may be, would force any new Quebec government to begin harvesting these resources, thrusting itself into the vanguard of the world's oil-rich nations and in the process relieve the ROC of a tremendous financial burden.

In fact, you can be almost certain the day Quebec does not have to share the riches from their oil and gas with Canadians is the day they'll start to drill!

Far more riches lie beneath the feet of every Quebecer than they will ever be able to extract from Ottawa, a fact that will become a major selling point when the separatists begin their next round of referendum talk.

As I explained this to my wife the other day she remarked, " Lowell, keeping billions of dollars worth of oil and gas in reserve for yourself while crying poverty so you can extract billions from the rest of the country is a little like having your freezer stuffed with filet mignon as you plunder the food bank every week!"

I think she's got it exactly right!

Because of this and from the other facts and arguments I present here you will be hard pressed not to agree with me that now is the perfect time to wave a friendly goodbye to Quebec!

We will all be a lot richer—and I suspect, happier as well, when the inevitable occurs and we finally go our separate ways.

CHAPTER ONE

THAT WAS THEN

Hanging on my home office wall right behind me is a framed letter, dated June 12, 1969 from the Canadian Prime Minister's office signed by Pierre Trudeau. It's addressed to Terry Kielty, General Manager of Broadcasting Station CFRA, 150 Isabella Street Ottawa and states as follows:

Dear Mr. Kielty:

I would like to convey my congratulations to you and your colleagues at CFRA for your work in winning the ACRTF trophy.

I understand that the Association confers the award for the English language radio or television station that contributes the most comprehensive broadcasting "to foster the comprehension and support of the French fact's importance to the achievement of Canadian unity".

In their citation, the judges commented, "their editorials are a very good reflection of the French Canadian situation within Confederation".

Veuillez accepter mes felicitations.

Sincerement,

Pierre Trudeau

Since I wrote and broadcast the editorials referred to, the trophy was presented to me in a little ceremony, held as I recall, in a local pizza parlour. (CFRA at the time was nothing if not frugal!) An artist's bronze avante garde interpretation of the fleur de lis. The trophy, being particularly ugly, was long ago relegated to a dusty drawer someplace and can no longer be found. I blame my wife!

(ACRTF is the acronym for Association Canadienne de la Radio et de la Television de Langue Francis.)

Hanging on the wall just above my desk, in fact, staring me boldly in the face as I write this, is the now famous overhead picture of the Canadian Unity Rally showing a good chunk of the more than 100,000 who flocked to Montreal on October 27, 1995 to beg Quebec not to leave us. Prominent in the picture is a huge Canadian flag brought to the rally by a busload of patriots from Windsor. The flag is being passed along hand-to-hand over the heads of those jammed into the square. You've probably seen the picture. It's become a Canadian icon.

The rally, as most of you know, is generally credited with persuading sufficient numbers of Quebecers to vote "Non" to tip the scales in favour of the narrow federalist referendum victory which followed three days later. Polls conducted only days prior to the referendum indicated support for the "Oui" side as high as 55%.

The referendum question, October 30, 1995 was as follows: " Do you agree that Quebec should become sovereign after having made a formal offer to Canada for a new economic and political partnership within the scope of the bill respecting the future of Quebec and the agreement signed on June 12, 1995?" (You can see why we need the Clarity Act!)

The result was 2,362,648 "No" votes (50.58%) compared to 2,308,360 (49.42%) for the "Yes" side. Voter turnout was 93.52%.

I have always been proud of the role I played in the conception, organization and promotion of that rally and for more than 50 years as a broadcaster, journalist, businessman and author and yes for many years a resident of the province; I have fought with every means at my disposal to keep Quebec within Confederation. I made sure both my daughters are fluently bilingual.

On the air and in previous books I have referred to Quebec separation as "stepping into a black hole of uncertainty and danger!"

No longer!

CHAPTER TWO

THIS IS NOW!

That was then! This is now!

In the years since the "Unity Rally", as the scandals, the corruption, the constant demands, the continued discrimination against minorities piled up, one upon the other, I found myself increasingly frustrated until, one day, not long ago I awoke surprised to discover that I had come full circle and was now convinced that Quebec separation was inevitable and that, sadly, I just didn't care anymore.

More than that.

I never thought I would say anything like this but here goes.

I have now become convinced that this is the perfect time to begin waving a friendly goodbye to Quebec. Perhaps even a bit more than just a friendly goodbye—a little friendly push might be just what the doctor ordered!

When you read here about the kind of sacrifices other countries have made in order to achieve independence you really have to wonder what stops Quebec from bucking up its collective courage and taking the courageous route that so many other countries have followed.

You are hard pressed today to find any more than a tiny handful of countries where more than one language and culture have been able to co-exist in separate clearly defined areas such as exists with the Province of Quebec.

Could it be that Quebec has allowed itself to be bribed into stepping back from the kind of independence that the people in places like the United States, Ireland, Hungary, the Czech Republic, Slovakia, the Balkan states, etc. even Scotland have fought and died for?

Why do I think now is the time to wave a friendly goodbye? Maybe even a friendly push?

Good questions. The answers are becoming more obvious every day.

Chief among those answers is—because finally the divorce can be amicable! If guys like me, who used to care very much about national unity, have lost patience with Quebec and are ready to throw in the towel, I suspect there are many others who feel exactly the same. A suspicion that, as far as I am concerned, has subsequently been proven accurate.

If you don't believe me, read some of the comments that have poured across my desk in recent months from more than 90 different Canadians from coast to coast!

Quebec separation back in 1995 would have been a recipe for disaster. Perhaps even violence. Passions were inflamed back then. The Cree Indians of northern Quebec were threatening war. The Pontiac and other predominantly Anglo sections of the Province were talking about holding their own separation referendums. "If Quebec can unilaterally separate from Canada", western Quebec callers to my show thundered "then we can separate from Quebec!"

In 1995, despite the constant separatist agitation we were, for the most part, a nation that still cared enough about each other to try and make the marriage work. There was still a good deal of affection even love on both sides. Car bumpers sported stickers proclaiming, "My

Country Includes Quebec." Close to 100,000 of us showed up to demonstrate that affection, that love, in Montreal's Place du Canada.

The overwhelming majority of callers to my show prior to the 1995 referendum were passionate in their insistence that we stay together as a nation. Some were in tears as they begged Quebeckers not to vote "Yes".

As referendum day approached, the nation held its breath. Some of our churches held special prayer vigils.

And in the end a majority (albeit very slim) of Quebeckers voted for the second time to stay together.

That was then! This is now!

You don't see any of those "My Country Includes Quebec" bumper stickers or T- shirts anymore.

Nor will we ever see 100,000 anxious Canadians gathering anywhere in an effort to persuade Quebeckers not to leave us. Those days are over.

If that rally were held today I doubt very much if a thousand would show up.

CHAPTER THREE

SAME OLD! SAME OLD!

One of those who took that pilgrimage to Montreal that fateful October day in 1995 is Jimmy Wainman of Orillia, a distant relative. He loaded up his old Oldsmobile with four buddies, two large Canadian flags and a bullhorn and headed east.

"We wanted to tell those frenchies not to leave cause we could always work things out. We got the words to that song Al-you-etta—practiced it a bit until, to tell the truth, we sounded pretty good, then took the bullhorn along with us to Montreal, fully intending to stir up a good old sing song that we could all join in on. We never got to sing the song or use the bullhorn but we were proud just to be there, taking part in what we thought was a pretty important bit of Canadian history. Orillia in the vanguard so to speak!"

"Jimmy," I asked, "Would you do it again?" He looked kind of sheepish for a moment. "Nah, I got to admit I really don't care that much anymore. I don't suppose today we'd be able to scratch up a carload to drive to Barrie to keep Quebec from leaving." He looked at me with a half grin. "We could probably fill a bus or two though if the rally was to boot them out!"

When pressed, he admitted there wasn't anything in particular that had changed his mind although the last election which saw the Parti Quebecois come back to power seemed to be the final straw. " Just got tired of the same old, same old," he said. "And all that corruption, man it's enough to drive you nuts!"

I had suspected that the word bilingualism might crop up in our conversation, but it never did until I raised the question. "Bilingualism? Not really, " shaking his head, "Here in Orillia bilingualism doesn't affect us. To be honest I don't think most of us up here in this part of Ontario give a damn about bilingualism. I know it's an issue for you there in Ottawa but up here no one speaks French or has any need to. It's not much of an issue really."

He then comes back to his original theme. "Nope, it's just we're tired of all the same old, same old from Quebec. You know, I've always said if you don't like the partner you're dancing with, then for goodness sake, change partners! Probably you'll both be a heck of a lot happier."

Jimmy is my no means alone in changing his mind and suggesting that a change of dance partners might make everyone a lot happier.

I've asked several callers and friends who made that Unity Rally trip to Montreal the same question. Would you do it again? The answer is always the same. "No, sadly I would not." This response, by the way, comes from several of the key organizers of the rally. Some of those I questioned have specific complaints, chief among them the whole issue of bilingualism, but for the most part it all boils down to the fact that the passion they once felt for national unity has been displaced by indifference and weariness.

One of the most common responses I get when I ask why they have changed their minds is a simple shrug of their shoulders. As in the case of Jimmy Wainman they just don't care anymore.

There was a time when setting the phone lines ablaze on my radio show was easy. Just toss out a few words like, "Quebec sovereignty," "Quebec separation" and you were guaranteed two hours of heated debate. It was almost like dropping a nice fat fly into a pool of starving trout. All dashing to the bait! Not today. Oh you'll still get a few calls about a French voice answering the phone at City Hall, or mandated French signs in Greely, but even those calls lack the kind of passion we used to see.

But the threat of Quebec separation? Sorry, Nothing but dead phones.

Well that's not entirely true. It all depends upon how you phrase the question.

CHAPTER FOUR

WOULD YOU TAKE THAT TRIP TO MONTREAL AGAIN?

On March 18, 2013, with the Charbonneau anti-corruption inquiry at full throttle, I decided to test the waters a bit with a different kind of question on the Lowell Green Show.

"Be honest with me," I said. "If Quebec, for whatever reason, decided to leave Confederation would you really care?" I went on to say, "I'd really like to hear from some of you who took that trip to Montreal back on October 27,1995. Given similar circumstances would you do it again?"

If ever there was any doubt that another "Unity Rally" would fizzle out, it was surely dispelled during the next two hours. And again the next day. Even the few callers who professed they still cared enough to take that trip to Montreal once more, confessed to becoming as one caller expressed it "battle weary."

But for the most part callers agreed with me that there may have been a time when they were willing to sport bumper stickers saying "My Country Includes Quebec", but that no longer is the case. Some callers, as you might expect, launched into anti-Quebec, or anti-bilingual rants, but for the most part you could sense that the callers were just like Jimmy Wainman, tired of the same old, same old and had finally come to the conclusion that an amicable divorce might be best for all.

The following with some editing for length, spelling and grammar, is a cross section of emails I received following the March 18 show. Only when the author provided specific permission to use their full name have I done so.

VOICES

No, I do not care if they separate—just let them do their thing—with no help from the rest of us. Thanks.

Joyce T, Ottawa, ON

~ • ~

I moved from Montreal to Ottawa almost five years ago because I was fed up with mismanagement at both the municipal and provincial levels. Quebec boasts a relatively low unemployment rate, but that's because one of every six workers in Quebec works for some level of government. That's 16 times (per capita) the number of civil servants in California and the highest ratio in North America. This is not sustainable in a province that can't even provide the services that should be associated with such a large public service. My first language is French and I do appreciate what Quebec has done to protect the French language. But this has gone too far.

Walter R, Ottawa, ON

~ • ~

I believe it is long overdue that Quebec leaves Canada. In my view it is unfortunate that Quebec didn't leave during Rene Levesque's day. Certainly the economic uncertainty would be all over by now and the taxpayers would have been spared billions upon billions of money trying to appease Quebec. Allowing Quebec to stay this long has only served to help them gain the maximum advantage over the years for when they do separate which is inevitable.

Louise H, Ottawa, ON

~ • ~

Are you kidding me? Every day I commute to work through China Town then past the Greek area, followed by Little Italy. Do you really think anyone around here gives a damn what happens with Quebec? Let's face it, in Toronto these days we're too busy trying to figure out the dozens of different languages on our storefronts while fighting the world's worst traffic to worry about Quebec. Give me a break!

Ansell Wilmott, Toronto, ON

~ • ~

The sooner they leave the better!

Rick T, Ottawa, ON

~ • ~

I am a 24-year-old white educated Anglophone male. I have never lived in a Canada where Anglophones had the same rights as our Francophone brothers; as a matter of fact I have never had the privilege of seeing the Quebec "nation" as an integral part of Canada. My generation has grown up seeing our political leaders do nothing but pander and surrender to the separatists' demands. Usually this resulted in using the rest of Canada's tax dollars to advance their apartheid-like anti-Anglophone agenda.

I've grown up feeling like a second-class citizen in my own country. I've never lived in an era where Quebec contributed to Canada or showed gratitude to the rest of Canada. I have never known, nor will my children know, a Canada that includes Quebec, for whether the province is within Canada's political boundaries, the Quebecois (with the help of our political leadership) has made it clear that Quebec is NOT part of Canada. This is why I believe it is time to wish Quebec a well-earned farewell!

Darius Campeau, Carleton Place, ON

~ • ~

Quebec is ready for separation. Canada should begin negotiations to agree on what conditions to implement the process. It has been a never-ending theme since 1970. Quebecers always have followed the philosophy that "We want more in order to stay." No more drain on the Canadian economy. I do not agree that we should have a European Union kind of agreement when they go. We should do the same as Czechoslovakia did. A straight split with no strings attached.

Vince from Alajuela, Costa Rica

~ • ~

I am not prepared to abandon Quebec just yet and I am surprised you are. You have always been such a staunch defender of Quebec and its role in Confederation. What in the world has happened to you? I understand your frustration. I am frustrated as well, but we need Quebec, if for no other reason than to differentiate ourselves from the Americans.

Helen Smithson, Collingwood, ON

~ • ~

I believe it is inevitable that Quebec will separate from Canada. Yes I have "French" fatigue. It would save the rest of Canada billions of dollars in transfer payments. I feel absolutely no animosity—I'm just tired. A divorce can be done amicably with the English. But I don't know about the native Canadians! Hummmmm.

Caroline A, Ottawa, ON

~ • ~

Let me tell you out here in flatland Saskatchewan no one gives a grain of barley what happens in Quebec. We wouldn't mind a bit of a thank you for all the money we poor farmers out here are shipping off for seven-dollar daycare in Quebec. Spent some time a few years ago in the Pontiac area. Great people but of course they'll still be there after separation. Heck, if not they are more than welcome to come out here to God's country. I could use a couple more deck hands during harvest.

Farmer George Cross, Battleford, SK

~ • ~

My simple opinion. Take your share of the Federal debt. Leave our Ontario healthcare and jobs alone and leave—see ya.

Serge, heart transplant recipient, Ottawa, ON

~ • ~

October 27,1995, I heard the call. I was there in Place du Canada proudly waving my Canadian flag hoping against hope that enough of my fellow Canadians in Quebec could see and hear how much we wanted them to continue to be part of our wonderful Canadian family. Would I do it again? Yes in a heartbeat. I know all the frustrations, the demands for more and more, but don't you think that a good bit of the responsibility for all of that rests with Federal Governments which over the years have given Quebec just about everything they wanted? I mean, come on. If all you had to do in order to get a nice new swimming pool at your house was throw a snit you'd be throwing snits all over the place. If we in the rest of Canada are willing to pour tens of billions of dollars into that province why would the province not rush to accept it all?

We still need Quebec. It's part of Canada and I hope it always will be, but I do agree the time has come to stop the transfer payments to all provinces and insist that they get their acts together, their books in order and as the Scottish leader says—stand on their own two feet!

Sharon W.T., Kanata, ON

~ • ~

I've just dumped a few gallons of crazy glue in the Ottawa River. That should keep our provinces together!

Terry Toll, Campbells Bay, QC

~ • ~

Would I care if Quebec were to become an independent nation? Good question, and I've done a lot of thinking about it. I suspect that number one, separation is inevitable. I mean can you name me a single nation in the world that is able to successful encompass more than one language or even more to the point more than one distinct culture? Look at all the other countries that have hived off separate, independent nations. Ireland, Czechoslovakia, the Balkans, half of Africa, and now even Scotland looks like it wants to march off to its own bagpipes! Could it be accomplished without rancour, without violence? I think so. Good heavens, the Czech Republic and Slovakia managed to go their separate ways with no fighting and they had a much tougher job defining borders than we would today with Quebec.

And I must confess I agree with you that attitudes have changed in the rest of Canada. A few years ago we would have been mad as hell if Quebec voted to separate, but today I suspect most of us wouldn't mind at all, although I've go to tell you down here in South Western Ontario we're much more concerned about those damned big windmills they keep planting on our farms than we are about the fate of Quebec.

Gerald Poirier, Forest, ON

~ • ~

Lowell I could not care less if Quebec decided to leave Canada, just so long as I could still buy cheap beer and bring it back to Ottawa!

R.B. Ottawa, ON

~ • ~

Two or three years ago, I suggested to you that all of Canada should hold a referendum about Quebec separating. I predicted that such a vote across the country would result in Quebec separating. You seemed quite put out by the idea at the time. I still believe that there should be another referendum only with all Canadians voting. That way we'd finally get rid of that festering sore called Quebec, that's sucking so much of our resources in an attempt to sustain it.

Ken McNairn, Ottawa, ON

~ • ~

Quebec: No it would not bother me at all. I say go. I am a separatist from Ottawa. So yes please go. They have already left culturally so all we have to do is count up the money they owe us. Imagine; we could have a foreign country on the other side of the river. We could use our passports to go to the casino. Good luck. I'll get some maudit beer and poutine in celebration and update my passport.

Jeremy Swanson, Ottawa, ON

~ • ~

I don't know what's wrong with you people up there in Ottawa. Of course we would all care very much if Quebec were to ever leave Canada. My Canada always includes Quebec and you people who think otherwise should all be ashamed of yourselves.

Annie Green, Mississauga ON

~ • ~

I would support Quebec leaving, but not from the position of the advantage to Quebec and their aspirations. I say this only from the perspective of the weariness of their griping and the great cost to Canada. Not just financial cost, but the psychology of having always to deal with a spoiled child. Time to cut the child loose.

Doug K, Ottawa, ON

~ • ~

Mr. Green, I find your comments intriguing to say the least. I think you have not fully researched the implications of Quebec separation. As a resident of Atlantic Canada we have thought about it long and hard, probably more so than most Canadians. I believe it could mean the end of Canada. Probably not tomorrow but certainly within ten years (two election cycles) Note: This has nothing to do with party affiliation, but with geography and history.

Atlantic Canada would not survive. We would seek closer ties with the northeastern United States. If you know our history, the Atlantic Provinces have always had a special relationship with the northeastern U.S. This relationship would be strengthened and would lead to some sort of economic and perhaps political union with the U.S. In fact, I believe the U.S. would seek it.

I ask you what would happen to the French populations in New Brunswick, northern Ontario and Manitoba? While they are quiet today, I ask you would the West still support a bilingual country? I think we both know the answer to that question. Then these populations will become more vocal and more isolated.

I think the center of power will shift to the West. Ontario will feel more isolated. I think Ontario will probably move to go its own way very quickly.

No, Mr. Green, we need one another. What we need is a political leader be he or she Liberal, Conservative, NDP or some other, maybe Canada Party who will take on this problem. The last political leader who did was PM Trudeau and he was vilified. We need someone with a vision who thinks of all of Canada and not its individual parts. We need to look at this in our universities and resolve it or Canada, as we know it will disappear and the world will be a poorer place.

Michael C, Atlantic Canada

~ • ~

For those Canadians who still worry about Quebec separating from Canada and becoming an independent country, it has essentially already happened. The only real obstacle to full Quebec independence is that we insist that they pay their own bills. As you know the rest of Canada will pour almost $8 billion into that province as part of the Federal Government's support via our famous transfer payments. What does the rest of Canada get in turn for this? You tell me!

Mark Kerr, Ottawa, ON

~ • ~

We are overdue in cancelling dual citizenships in Canada so I believe a week after Quebec separates would be the perfect time to do that. It would give more meaning to Quebecer votes then. I don't want Quebec influencing us after they are gone.

Pete M, Brockville, ON

~ • ~

When Quebec separates in order to protect their culture, it will then become a precedent for the rest of Canada to take similar steps to protect our language and culture. It is insanity for people to dilute their own culture to the point of extinction. Quebec knows this and let us in the rest of Canada cheer their hopeful future which ultimately will be ours.

Mike Rowe, Nepean, ON

~ • ~

For some time I, and many others, have concluded that we should encourage Quebec to separate. However, it is the terms and conditions that are important to the rest of Canada as well as groups within Quebec such at the Cree Indians.

The Crees have already declared that they would stay within Canada and that they would take over the LeGrande hydro project and if necessary temporarily disable it in a non-destructive manner. I am privy to their plan.

The borders would have to be returned to where they were prior to Quebec joining Canada and the St. Lawrence Seaway would remain within Canada. All transfer payments would cease.

All military bases in Quebec would be closed and transfers made available to all, including Quebecers who swear loyalty to Canada.

There are many other issues to be negotiated but these are some of the more obvious and crucial items.

Michael in Barrhaven, ON

~ • ~

I lived in Gatineau for many years and saw the writing on the wall in 2003. It was time to leave. I have family still there, my son married a Quebecer and their home language is French. I speak to my granddaughter in English and maybe she will eventually be able to speak English. I say it is time to cut the apron strings and let the province go and grow up. Let the province take care it itself, financially and emotionally.

Kay Matthews, Ottawa, ON

~ • ~

I think Quebec should separate, always have. But for reasons I have never heard anyone mention. We have grown as a country, similar to a family. Today, just as with children, Quebec has grown strong and mature enough to stand on her own. One advantage would be that English-speaking people would finally be able to get a job with their own government.

Yarrum, Kanata, ON

~ • ~

Tyler here. Yes Lowell, it is time for them to go! They hate us and it is a slap in the face every minute they remain part of Canada.

Tyler Buglar, Ottawa, ON

~ • ~

I agree with Quebec separation, but for different reasons than you and your listeners have stated. I want Quebec to become a proud and independent nation since that is the only way we can preserve our language and culture.

You in English Canada obviously don't care as much about your culture as we do in Quebec since you have allowed yourself to become diluted to the point where in some cities—Vancouver for example—English is now the second language. We will not allow that to happen in Quebec. Here we are adamant that we will preserve and enhance our language and culture. If the rest of Canada doesn't care about its heritage that's too bad for you, but we are not going to be caught in the same self-defeating trap.

James Morris, Ste. Jerome, QC

~ • ~

As someone who was born in Montreal and left the province in 2005, I can safely say that not only will Canada not mind Quebec separation, but many Canadians would vote to expel the province from Confederation. Quebec is normally labeled as a progressive state, but in reality, it is the most regressive state in the free world. The province enacts laws that restrict education, restrict innovation and promote discrimination. We as a nation celebrate equality, justice, fairness to all—concepts shockingly absent from Quebec. My opinion: Hand them their hat and show them the door.

Arron K, Pembroke, ON

~ • ~

Yes French speaking Quebecers are entitled to be concerned about the survival of their language and culture. But not at the expense of trampling others' rights.

Bryan K, Ottawa, ON

~ • ~

I heard you suggest that with separation, Quebec minorities might not face as much discrimination. You make an interesting point, although, fact is we cannot be sure. There is no question that in some quarters there is a genuine dislike, sometimes even a hatred of minorities, especially the English speaking kind, but it is also true that in the minds of many Quebecers their only concern is the preservation of their language and culture.

If Quebec became an independent nation there is no question the need to drive the Anglos out of the province would be lessened considerably. In fact it can be argued that once Quebec achieves total control over its own nation, Anglos will be much more welcome. That's presuming of course that good will and some common sense survive. Not much of that these days, sadly in Quebec.

Andre Cadotte, Montreal, QC

~ • ~

Lowell, Quebec is already gone. Quebec has its own civil code, has not signed onto the Constitution, or the Canada Health Act. It controls its own immigration as well as representing itself on many entities of the UN such as UNESCO. The only difference is that it doesn't have an anthem and has someone else paying the bills.

On the financial side nothing will change. Transfer payments will be renamed foreign aid and bilingualism policy won't change because the Franco-Ontarians will form the new beachhead for French culture preservation. All government departments whether federal, provincial or municipal will still promote bilingualism. So what is new to care or not care about? I do find it bizarre however that Canada would cede all of the Quebec territory to that new nation, which would be contrary to the Ungava Treaty.

John K, Ottawa, ON

~ • ~

My feeling Lowell is that I really don't care anymore. They can keep their culture and language but official bilingualism in the rest of Canada must be scrapped as it is ruining our country. You say that those in a separated Quebec could still have dual citizenship and a Canadian passport. Does this mean that these individuals could still come into the rest of Canada, work for the federal government, and take jobs away from the rest of Canadians like they do now in our hospitals, building trades, etc. just because they are bilingual? And with dual citizenship would they be allowed to run for Parliament and even become Prime Minister of Canada? That would be going too far in my opinion.

Deacon Moran McMahon, Orleans, ON

~ • ~

We're talking about the potential breakup of the best country in the world. How could anybody in his or her right mind not care? Shame on those who don't care!

Jim H. sent from an iPhone

~ • ~

Lowell, whatever happens, this time all Canadians must be given the opportunity to have a say. On two occasions in the past it has been Quebec and Quebec alone that was allowed to determine the fate of the entire country. No more. The next time we all get a say—we all get a vote. No more tail wagging the dog!

Ann Gravelle, Gatineau, QC

~ • ~

Often it seems like Quebec is the tail wagging the dog. I live in Ontario and one does get fed up with what goes on in Quebec and their demands to the rest of Canada. I don't like how they treat the Anglophones either. There seems to be this double standard.

From their standpoint they may be sadly surprised if they ever do get their independence. They will probably have even less say in trade with

Canada and the U. S. There is one common analogy about Canada in bed with the elephant next door. (The U.S.) We know how that often works out! You make the analogy about an amicable divorce, but Quebec may end up pining for the old girlfriend they gave up!

George C, Ottawa, ON

~ • ~

I'm all for a divorce just so long as Quebec doesn't get the gold mine and Canada gets the shaft!

Lindsay M, Carp, ON

~ • ~

No, I do not want Quebec to leave UNLESS it means that the Official Languages Act is dropped across Canada.

In Eastern Ontario, "Cultural Inventories", Linguistic Roadmaps" and "Bilingual Sign" bylaws are all indicators that the Quebec separatists have taken over Eastern Ontario.

Quebec license plates in so many institutions are also indications that even if Quebec separated, if they are allowed to continue to work in Ontario, what progress will have been made? Our English speaking young people are fleeing to work in the West while Quebec youth take Ontario jobs and tax dollars back to Quebec.

French only health clinics, French only community centers, French only hospitals, French only senior living centers. If you think that by Québec separating there will be peace, you are wrong.

Yesterday, Canadians for Language Fairness had our 2nd Annual St. Patrick's Day Brunch (A sellout, 120 people) and the resentment, anger and frustration was incredible in particular the following complaints:

Jobs being based on language not skills.

Families being broken up because young adults are being forced to find jobs out West or in the USA.

Legal challenges being heard by "activist" judges (Judge Monique Metivier).

French immersion that has failed our children.

Language Commissioner Graham Fraser refusing to meet with a Canada-wide organization that represents victims of forced bilingualism.

As of January 1, 2013, every municipality in Ontario must provide bilingual services no matter how few unilingual Francophones are in their communities.

So much for freedom of speech. The unrestricted use of the English language is now against the law in Eastern Ontario municipalities.

The question should not be whether Quebec separates. The question should be whether forced bilingualism and language laws are an attack on our inalienable right to freedom of speech!

Beth Trudeau, Spokesperson, Canadians for Language Fairness, Embrun, ON

~ • ~

It isn't just on my program that similar sentiments are being expressed. The following letter to the editor appeared in the National Post on June 5, 2013. It was written in response to an earlier comment by Dan Delmar that the only people upset with the situation in Quebec today are what Delmar called Angryphones.

The following is the reply by Richard D. Field of Toronto:

"It is unfortunate that Dan Delmar cannot comprehend that nearly one million English-speaking Canadians have left Quebec since the French-first language laws came on the scene. The trick word "Angryphone" is just that, a comedic response by the Anglo appeasers that stayed and did not fight for their rights against the Franco chest-thumpers that delighted in rubbing their Anglo fellow citizens' noses in the dirt of Quebec's myopic provincialism.

Howard Galganov's life was threatened and his property destroyed by the cowardly Quebecois linguistic fanatics. He moved to Ontario to continue his fight. He fought for 14 years in Quebec and had damn little support from the Anglo community. He is a courageous Canadian.

Why doesn't the National Post write an article, exploring why Anglophones cannot hold senior positions in the federal civil service or Crown corporations, or rise above the rank of major in the military if they cannot speak French patois (as judged by a French-patois hiring panel.) Having a French last name even helps.

English only speakers are now a disenfranchised sub-class of Canadian citizenry.

This is one sick country!
Richard D. Field, Toronto, ON

~ • ~

And then there was this dandy little tirade that appeared in the letters to the editor section of the National Post, June 5, 2013. It was written in response to Radio Canada's decision (since rescinded) to become simply "ICI".

Heritage Minister James Moore warns that Canadians won't tolerate any move away from a pan-Canadian identity. While this may be the government's position, it is unlikely that Canadians feel this way.

Most Canadians wish Quebec would separate, to end the continual distraction and right what has become an unfair situation. Canada's government and laws are tilted in favour of Quebec to the point that most Canadians feel the treatment to appease Quebec (e.g., unequal representation in the Senate and the Supreme Court, official bilingualism, transfer payments, disproportionate cultural grants, etc.) has resulted in unfairness.

While Quebec was treated badly in English-Canada in the past, the means used to redress that situation have been excessive, resulting in an inequitable situation for Canadians outside Quebec.

Perhaps a national referendum would be appropriate.

Mac Walker, Edmonton, AB

~ • ~

In all, I received more than 200 emails and phone calls from that one two-hour program. At least 90 per cent of them indicated that my assumptions were correct, they would not seriously regret the loss of Quebec. Some, as you can see, still hold grievances, particularly as it applies to what they deem to be "forced bilingualism", but for the most part it's primarily a matter of just losing patience with the constant demands.

The sentiments expressed to me in the phone calls, the emails and from people who stopped me on the street following the program are perhaps best summed up by this hand written letter that arrived just the other day from Surrey, BC

"Lowell", "you and I have never met, but in listening to you the other day as you discussed the issue of Quebec and its role in Canada, I couldn't help but hear some anguish in your voice. You said, and I believe you, that you are totally frustrated with all the problems that Quebec continues to present. The corruption, the constant demands for more money, for more special treatment, etc. etc. You are perfectly correct we are all getting very tired of it.

But I also sensed that in some way you are also sad. No doubt the fact that you have worked so hard for so long to try and keep Quebec within Confederation plays a role in your reaction to what's happening and how you feel about it. No one likes to lose. I understand that many members of your family, even your daughter and granddaughter still live in the province. This must make it even harder for you.

What you should know is that you are not alone. There was a time when I and all members of my very large family out here on the west coast were adamant federalists. We didn't go to Montreal in 1995, some of us weren't even alive then, but several of us did drive around with those famous bumper stickers saying, "My Canada includes Quebec". But, sadly, just like you, we have all come to the same conclusion. Quebec will never be happy in Confederation no matter what benefits it receives from the rest of Canada.

Lowell we tried to convince Quebec to stay. We used every means in our power to keep them in Confederation. But let's be very honest here, for all the money and other benefits we poured into that province we never once heard a thank you, or even an acknowledgment—only complaints and demands for more.

At the very least now that you have conducted your programs on the matter, tapped into the sentiment outside Quebec and written a book about it, a few Quebecers will begin to understand that we have lost patience, certainly out here in the west. We tried, we gave and gave and gave and received precious little in return. There's a limit to our patience and at least around here that limit has been reached.

I've conducted a little poll out here among friends and family and without exception we all agree with you. Let's start the process towards a very friendly parting of the ways. No bitterness please; no recriminations. We've all shared a very long, sometimes bumpy road together so now that that road is coming to an end, let's sit down in good faith, both sides and work out an agreement that, while it will never be perfect, at least lets us be good friends after all is said and done.

Other countries around the world have managed to cut the apron strings and are happier now that they have become independent nations. Maybe the same will hold true for Quebec and Canada.

We'll still be living side by side. We'll still need to trade with each other, but as you said more than once on your program, maybe, just like some of us who have divorced, maybe we can be better friends after the divorce than we ever were before. A sweet dream, I know. There will be problems, but we're a good people we Canadians, we can work it out. But you are right, it is kind of sad. Could the great experiment of two languages, two cultures have worked out? We will never know.

Shirley Westover. Surrey, BC

~ • ~

I don't doubt for a moment that there still a kind of wistful affection percolating amidst our two solitudes, I detect that sentiment in much of the correspondence, but as with a middle aged couple that has been bitterly feuding for decades the passion, the ability to wound, even to disappoint is gone. In relationships such as those, scant attention is paid to anything that is said or done. A document may claim they are still married, but in reality each goes their own separate way, living semi-independent lives, bound together only by economics, apathy and inertia. If they were still hurting each other they would consider divorce, but why bother?

Fact is, if they did bother to get a divorce there's a good chance they might become, if not lovers again, at least friends. Who among us doesn't know at least one couple that will readily admit that they are better friends today, after the divorce, than they ever were when married? It works that way with some nations as well. The Republic of Ireland springs immediately to mind, but there are other, perhaps even better examples of where a national breakup has ended centuries of animosity, feuding and fighting and made way to good solid friendships.

For example, Scotland and England.

CHAPTER FIVE

HISTORY TELLS US QUEBEC SEPARATION IS INEVITABLE

On June 23rd and 24th, 1314, an army of Scots under Robert de Bruce defeated a much larger English force led by King Edward II at the battle of Bannockburn in central Scotland.

It was here that Sir Henry de Bohun galloped ahead of the advancing English army to challenge the Scots King Robert de Bruce to single combat, one of the most historic events in the almost thousand year war for Scottish independence.

According to The Scottish National Archives records:

"Robert de Bruce rode forward to meet de Bohun who was fully armoured with lance and shield and rode a heavy destrier horse. De Bruce had a much smaller horse and was armed only with a sword and short axe. De Bohun rode at de Bruce with lance couched. De Bruce evaded de Bohun's lance point and as the English knight thundered past he struck a deadly blow to his head with his axe."

De Bohun fell dead demoralizing the English troops who were subsequently slaughtered as they fled.

King Edward managed to escape.

For the Scots it remains to this day the most famous of all the countless battles fought over the centuries for Scottish independence.

What the Scots would sooner forget is what happened about 200 years after the Battle of Bannockburn.

On September 9, 1513 an army of about 20,000 men led by King James IV of Scotland invaded England in response to several provocations including warrants issued by Catherine of Aragon, the Regent in England, to seize all the property of Scotsmen in England.

The Scottish army was met by the English commanded by the Earl of Surrey at what is today know as the Battle of Flodden, or Flodden Field.

It was a terrible disaster for the Scots. King James was killed in battle along with many of the most important noblemen of the day. Total Scottish losses were about 12,000 killed. The English lost 1,500 men killed.

It was the largest battle ever fought between the two kingdoms. Historians describe it as the last great medieval battle in the British Isles. And the last battle on the British Isles during which a monarch was killed.

The battlefield still looks today much as is probably did at the time of the battle. but the burn and marsh that badly hampered the Scots' advance is now drained. A monument, erected in 1910 is easily reached from Branston Village by following the road past St. Paul's Church. There is a small car park and a clearly marked and signposted trail with interpretive boards making it easy to visualize the battle.

Each year, the neighbouring Scottish town of Coldstream marks the Battle of Flodden by a traditional horse-ride to the battlefield and then a church service to mark all those men who perished during the fight. This is held during the first week of August.

Since 2008 plans have been underway to mark the Quincentennial of the battle on or before the 9th of September 2013.

It was not until May 1, 1707 that the blood being shed between England and Scotland ended when England, Ireland and Scotland joined together to form the Parliament of Great Britain. At which point, of course the bloodshed began between England and Ireland but that's another chapter.

What's important to understand is that while the Scottish war of independence left the battlefields in 1707, the dream of independence, in Scotland just as in Quebec remains very much alive for many.

Humiliation draws a long bow. Scotland has Flodden Field— Quebec the Plains of Abraham!

And just as in Quebec, Scotland has elected a separatist party to power. The Scottish National Party (SNP) lead by Alex Salmon won an unprecedented majority in 2011 and has announced that a separation referendum will be held on September 18, 2014. The question will be "Should Scotland be an independent country?"

Will Scotland be able to win what a thousand years of battles could not? A safe and secure independent nation? Only time will tell of course but just as with Quebec what is happening in Scotland is a powerful reminder that for a proud people, dreams of independence never die!

One of the really amazing things about the movement for Scottish independence is, unlike the situation involving Quebec, there is no issue of language in the British Isles. Since the 17th century the predominant language in both Scotland and England has been English (okay with different accents).

More than that, the English and Scots, for the most part share an ancestral heritage. Both groups spring from the same Anglo/Saxon roots with a sprinkling of Picts and Norse with Norman blood tossed in for good measure.

When you consider that the Scots and the Brits have been feuding and fighting for more than a thousand years and may soon separate despite sharing a common language, a similar culture and virtually the same ancestry you are forced to wonder how in the world Quebec and

Canada, with all the differences we have, managed to stick together as long as we have. And even more to the point. How much longer can we hold it together?

Scottish leader Alex Salmond says Scots should, "Speak with our voice. Independence will be a day when Scotland takes responsibility for our country, when we are able to choose our own direction and contribute in our own distinct way. It will provide us with a new, more modern relationship with other nations and Britain. A 'no' vote means a future of governments we don't vote for, imposing cuts and policies we didn't support. A 'yes' vote means a future where we can be absolutely certain, 100 per cent certain, that the people of Scotland will get the government they vote for!

Independence Day will be the day we stand on our own two feet." (Does any of this sound familiar?)

The Scottish opposition Labour Party and the British Government are fighting hard for a "no" vote, and as in the case of Quebec are using, as their major weapons, the threat of economic chaos with separation.

Most observers however believe that in the end history may provide the deciding factor in Scotland and in Quebec!

And as an added reminder of how important history may be, consider the fact that the Scottish referendum will be held in 2014 during the height of celebrations to mark the 700th anniversary of the greatest victory in Scottish history—the Battle of Bannockburn.

CHAPTER SIX

INDEPENDENCE—IT'S BRED IN THE BONE!

The announcement concerning a referendum for Scottish independence was made on March 21, 2013. Two days later I received this very interesting and thoughtful email:

"Lowell, we should not be surprised by the Scottish move towards separation, nor for that matter, the on-going agitation for independence that's been at the forefront of Canadian politics almost since Confederation.

Fact is, the desire for independence is universal. Listen to the words being used by Alex Solmond when he tries to persuade his fellow Scots to take that big leap:

"The day we achieve independence is the day we are able to speak with our own voice, choose our own direction and contribute in our distinct way— the day we stand up on our own two feet—but not to stand alone."

Think about those words. Is there any among us who has not expressed the same thoughts perhaps even used the same words when explaining to our parents why it was time for us to leave home and strike out on our own? Or these days maybe it's the other way around and the parents are suggesting that maybe it's time for the twenty something son to move out of the basement and "stand on his own two feet!"

Yes, but with Scotland and Quebec we're not talking about individuals, we're talking about nations I hear you say. True, but it's not the rocks, the lakes, the mountains or the buildings of a country that seeks independence but the inhabitants, the most normal of whom seek the freedom to make their own decisions, to stand on their own two feet!"

So when you really stop to think about it. Perhaps we have been judging Quebec separatists too harshly in their desire to leave Canada. Could it be that we have been blind to the "bred in the bone" desire to as the Quebecois say, "Be masters in their own house"?

Perhaps what we should really be critical about is the fact that rather than boldly and courageously grasping the opportunity to achieve independence when it presented itself with the first referendum in 1980 and again in October of 1995 they "chickened" out. They talked the talk, but didn't have the guts to actually do the walk.

I say the desire for independence is natural and even courageous.

Not having the guts to actually take the step, but using the threat of leaving to hold the rest of the country to ransom is cowardly. Just as with the adult son who's afraid to leave mommy's cooking, maybe what's needed is a little bit of a push. Or perhaps a big one!

And as for the Scots I say: "Remember Braveheart!"

Helen Sinclair, Mississauga, ON

~ • ~

While, as you would expect, the bulk of the correspondence I receive comes from eastern Ontario and western Quebec this matter of Quebec independence prompted a much wider response than usual.

Thanks to the Internet and live streaming my show is now heard around the world and, as you can see from some of the emails and letters published here, opinion on national unity poured in from all parts of the country.

The following point of view from the West Coast is a typical example:

Lowell, there is no doubt in my mind that the book you wrote a couple years ago entitled "Mayday! Mayday! Curb Immigration, Stop Multiculturalism Or It's The End of the Canada We Know", played a role in our government's efforts to improve and modernize our immigration policies. I know from speaking to friends and relatives that the facts and arguments you presented opened many eyes and at least started the process of changing minds in this country.

It is surely no accident that many of the problems you pointed out in the book, the appeal process that can last decades, for example, have been modified or resolved.

I'm not suggesting that Immigration Minister Jason Kenney sat down, read your book and because of it, began to make major changes to our immigration policy. What I am saying is that information such as you provided in Mayday! Mayday! when widely distributed, helps to change public opinion that in turn prompts or perhaps allows governments to make needed changes in public policy.

While obviously I have not read this new book you are writing, I suspect it may and indeed I hope it will present facts and arguments that will, at the very least, encourage a national debate on the Quebec situation.

It seems to me that for far too long, the fate of Canada, the issue of national unity, has been left solely in the hands of one group of people, those who live in Quebec.

Hopefully your new book will, among other things, convince some of us that the time has come for all Canadians, not just Quebecers, to decide whether our relationship should continue as is, be modified, or perhaps even severed.

I am sure you are aware that in 2014 Canada must decide whether to renew the so called "equalization program" which benefits Quebec disproportionately. I suspect that if sufficient numbers of Canadians began to rebel over this incredible welfare scheme, that at the very least we could convince the government to either scrap the program entirely or implement policies that would force Quebec to stop draining the rest of the country and stand on its own two feet.

There is no reason whatsoever that Quebec should be a "have not" province given the James Bay Hydro Electric project and the incredible oil and gas resources they have recently discovered.

We need a national debate on whether we wish to continue pumping billions of dollars into Quebec with nothing but headaches as our reward! Hopefully Lowell, your new book will help launch just such a debate.

James Harrison, Vancouver, BC

CHAPTER SEVEN

THE CONVERSION

I said earlier that I awoke one morning to discover that I had come full circle from being a staunch supporter of Canadian unity to someone who believes it might be better for all concerned if Quebec were to leave. The fact is, of course that such a metamorphosis doesn't occur overnight. Unlike the Biblical account of Paul's travels, my conversion didn't occur on the road to Damascus, but began instead on a river cruise through countries once crushed by the weight of the "Iron Curtain".

The graphic evidence of the desperate struggle for freedom and independence that confronted us in Budapest was heart wrenching but in some strange way, at least for me, uplifting. Here was a city, a country, a people who suffered terribly at the hands of the Nazis, the Communists, the Fascists and the traitors in their midst. They were tortured, murdered and exiled by the tens of thousands but never gave up their dream, their fight to be free; to govern themselves.

Evidence of the horrors inflicted confronted us around almost every corner in downtown Budapest, but it wasn't until we entered the "Great Synagogue" that some of the affection and respect I had always had for the Quebecois began to slip away.

The synagogue (the largest in Europe) sits at the edge of what was once the few blocks of Budapest that served as the Jewish Ghetto into which were jammed some 70,000 Jews during the Nazi occupation. Of the between eight and ten thousand who died in the Ghetto (most of the rest were shipped to concentration camps) two thousand are buried in a mass gravesite (now a memorial) at the side of the synagogue.

At the rear of the building is a very moving metal sculpture of a willow tree whose leaves bear the names of all who died in the ghetto. Donated by movie actor Tony Curtis in memory of his Hungarian father the "willow tree" shares space with another memorial honouring 240 non-Jewish Hungarians who risked their lives to rescue Jews from the "death camps". One of those honored is Raoul Wallenberg, a Swedish diplomat who, by preparing special protective passports, is believed to have saved the lives of thousands.

As I bent down for a closer look at the memorials, an elderly man who was standing quietly nearby, cap in hand, turned to me and said, "So here we find the very worst that mankind is capable of," and pointed to the gravesite. Then nodding slightly in the direction of the Wallenberg memorial, "and the very best!"

It set me to thinking.

Nothing compares to the fate of European Jews under the Nazis, but as I left the "Great Synagogue" I couldn't help but wonder if perhaps Quebec Anglos could understand, better than most, the kind of discrimination and hatred that herded innocents into ghettos.

Of course the separatists and their camp followers didn't force anyone into a ghetto and they certainly didn't herd anyone into railcars on their way to death camps. But, and I know this will upset many of you, we cannot escape the fact that some 280,000 Anglos, along with another 80,000 Allophones were essentially herded out of the province in the face of extremely discriminatory, harassing and often hateful government edicts and actions.

Some may have left for other reasons, but there can be no doubt that in the overwhelming majority of cases, while not compelled to pin yellow stars to their jackets, people left the province because, as members of a very small minority, they were singled out, discriminated against, harassed and humiliated, not because of their religion, but because of their mother tongue!

Hitler wanted all Jews gone from Europe and set out to kill them all. Pauline Marois, just as with separatists before her, doesn't want Anglos dead, just not around where she has to see them or deal with them in Quebec.

Of course their methods are different, so too the motivation, but in the end both the separatists and the Nazis had and have one similar goal. No more Jews in Europe. No more Anglos in Quebec.

A harsh assessment? Yes. Unfair? Some will say so. But honestly, can there by any doubt that Hitler wanted to rid Europe of Jewry? Can there be any doubt that Pauline Marois and sadly many of her followers want to rid Quebec of anyone whose mother tongue is not French?

In the end it may very well turn out that Ms Marois will be more successful in her efforts than Hitler was with his.

Don't get me wrong, I am not suggesting the discrimination and repression that drove more than a quarter million people out of Quebec are in any way, shape or form comparable to the fate of Jews during the Holocaust. In fact you would be hard pressed to search history and find anything more evil than what the Nazis did to the Jews under Hitler and his henchmen.

But the visit to the "Great Synagogue " and similar examples of man's inhumanity to man that confronted us during our stay in Budapest drove home to me the realization that the difference between the Nazi's treatment of the Jews and Quebec's treatment of Anglos is really only a matter of degree.

Hitler and his henchmen wanted all Jews dead and set about to kill them . The Separatists want Anglos out of their province and set about to accomplish just that, not with guns and whips, but with pernicious laws and regulations and yes open, sometimes even legislated, bigotry!

So there can be no misunderstanding, I repeat, there is no comparison between the suffering imposed by the Holocaust and that which prompted the exodus of Anglos from Quebec, but what happened to the Anglos and continues to happen is nonetheless a result of government policies, that blatantly discriminate against a small minority on the basis of language.

Make no mistake, Quebec official treatment of Anglos is far from benign and has never really been properly exposed for the mean-spiritedness and outright bigotry that drives it.

Perhaps even worse, just as in Nazi Germany, much of the Quebec population turns a blind eye to what is glaringly evident to anyone who cares to see.

Sadly, there will be no memorials to Quebecers who fought against the injustice of it all!

What we experienced in the next two days in Budapest convinced me even more than it's bloody well time Quebec stops its cultural strangulation of Anglos, stops harassing its minorities, bucks up its courage, as most other countries worth there salt have done, and as the Scots in favour of independence say, "Stand on your own two feet!"

When you stop to think about it, you separatists, it's kind of gutless to hold Canada in contempt for not severing its last ties with the British Monarchy when you don't have the courage to sever your ties with Canada!

CHAPTER EIGHT

SHOES ON THE DANUBE

But the Danube is not blue," I say. "Ah," says our guide, eyes crinkling in a grin, "it's only blue for lovers!" Chuckles all round from out little band of Budapest exploring Canadians, then some loud snorts of laughter when one wise acre pipes up: "Hey it looks blue to me!" We continue our guided tour through the heart of Budapest. The magnificent Parliament Buildings to our left, the historic and very beautiful Chain Bridge ahead in the distance.

"What's this?" asks a woman strolling just ahead of us. "What are these iron shoes doing here?"

Our guide, suddenly somber, pauses for a moment. "Let me explain," he says." It's very sad." We gather in closer, the better to hear. Shocked but fascinated by what he is saying, I record the story he tells.

"Miklos Voglhut was, for many years, one of Hungary's most loved and most famous singers. He performed frequently in many of our most popular cabarets during what I think you call the roaring twenties. It was a time when anti-Semitism was sweeping across Hungary and the rest of Europe so he changed his name to Miklos Vig. Vig in Hungarian means cheerful or merry.

He made countless recordings and performed many times at the Budapest Operetta Theatre and Budapest Orpheum and became one of Hungary's first radio stars. He was beloved all around the country, the Frank Sinatra, if you like, of Hungary.

But In 1944, despite the fact he did not have a Jewish name and indeed had married into a Catholic family, our very own Hungarian Nazis—the Arrow Cross Party— rounded up Miklos along with many others from the Jewish ghetto. Like so many before him and many more after him, Miklos was forced to strip naked, take off his shoes on the banks of the Danube River, right here where we are standing now, then all were shot at close range so that they fell into the river and were washed away. This was common practice during 1944 and 1945.

What you see here along the banks of the Danube are 60 pairs of rusted shoes cast out of iron. As you can see they are shoes to reflect those styles being worn during those terrible years. And if you look closely you can see that no one was spared from the brutality of the Arrow Cross militia."

Some of us are in tears by this time, especially when we walk along what is called the "Shoes on the Danube" and can see children's shoes.

Our guide points to a high stone bench with these words inscribed in Hungarian, English and Hebrew:

"TO THE MEMORY OF THE VICTIMS SHOT INTO THE DANUBE BY ARROW CROSS MILITIMEN IN 1944-45. ERECTED APRIL 2005"

I will be frank with you. Of all the memorials, including even the one at Vimy the "Shoes on the Danube museum" of Budapest is the one that haunts me still from time to time.

It is what our guide says next that prompts me to include his "Shoes on the Danube" story in this book.

"If you would like to get a better idea of Hungary's struggle for freedom and independence," he tells us, "you should visit the 'House of Terror' which we call 'Terror Haza.'

Those words again—"the struggle for freedom and independence."

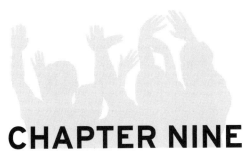

CHAPTER NINE

TERROR HAZA
(House of Terror)

Andrassy Boulevard is one of Budapest's most beautiful thoroughfares. Lined by stately apartment buildings and fashionable storefronts, it connects downtown Budapest and the Danube with "Heroes Square" where students tore down the giant statue of Stalin during the 1954 Hungarian Revolution. The street is named after one of the Austro-Hungarian Empire's greatest Hungarian statesmen, Count Gyula Andrassy.

There is little to distinguish 60 Andrassy Blvd from the other neo-renaissance buildings that surround it except for a small sign that states simply "TERROR HAZA".

Today 60 Andrassy is a museum. From 1937 until 1956 it was a house of unbelievable terror. A house of torture and murder.

Let me read directly from the visitor's guide handed out to those who today visit what the Hungarians describe as, " The statue of terror, a monument to the victims.

"The House of Terror" is a museum now, but it was witness to two shameful and tragic periods in Hungary's 20th century history. It was truly a house of terror.

In 1944, during the gruesome domination of the Hungarian Arrow Cross Party, this building, known as the "House of Loyalty" was the party headquarters of the Hungarian Nazis.

Then between 1945 and 1956, the notorious communist terror organization, the AVO and its successor, the AVH, took up residence here. 60 Andrassy Boulevard had become the house of terror and dread.

This museum commemorates the victims of terror, but it is also a memento, reminding us of the dreadful acts of terrorist dictatorships.

As the guide explained to us as we explored the museum, The Arrow Cross Party was a group of Hungarians that established a governing body to collaborate with the Nazis. "France had Vichy, we had the Arrow Cross," was the way he described it. "But the Arrow Cross was much more vicious, cruel and murderous than the Vichy Government of France. Any Jews still left in Hungary were killed or shipped off to concentration camps."

He reminded us of the "Shoe Museum" we had seen only yesterday.

"In 1944 near the end of the war," he explained, "many of us in Hungary wanted to end it. We wanted to surrender and try and reconstruct our lives. In response the Arrow Cross Party arrested thousands of us without warrants or charges. Many were taken to the basement of this building here at 60 Andrassy, tortured and killed."

He pointed to a sewer grill in the middle of the basement floor. "That was for the blood," he said.

According to our guide, even though the Nazis were near defeat, the Arrow Cross Party and their henchmen believed that Hitler would soon unleash a secret weapon, which would win the war for him, so thousands of teenaged boys were rounded up and sent to the Eastern Front to be massacred by the Russians.

In 1945, after the defeat of Hitler, one of the first things the Soviet occupiers did was take over 60 Andrassy Boulevard, establishing first the State Security Office (AVO) then the State Security Authority (AVH).

If possible the atrocities carried out at 60 Andrassy were even worse than under the Arrow Cross. "The officers serving at 60 Andrassy were masters of life and death, mostly death," said our guide.

Here is how the official guidebook of "Terror Haza" describes those terrible days under the Soviets.

"During the most unimaginable and horrific interrogations lasting for weeks, many of the victims died. Those who survived the body-crushing and soul-debasing pain were ready to sign any document.

A whole host of informers, a shadow army, watched people on factory floors, in editorial rooms, in offices, at universities, in churches and theatres, noting down their every move. These informers received full backing as well as ideological and practical guidance from the Soviet occupiers. No one could feel safe from them. It was with their support that the Communists came to power and built up and preserved their hegemony-a tyrannical regime that seized, mistreated or crippled one person from every third family In Hungary.

The visitors' guide concludes with these words:

"Until now the building blended in with the other houses along the boulevard. Now transformed into a museum, it not only pays tribute to the memory of the victims by housing the exhibition, but the exterior also conjures up its spirit. With its transformation, the "House of Terror" is no longer simply a building. 60 Andrassy Boulevard has become a sculpture in the shape of a building that is a monument to the victims.

The terror's former house demonstrates today that sacrifices made in the name of freedom are never futile. From the fight against the two murderous regimes, the powers of freedom and independence have emerged victorious.

Again those words—freedom and independence. Few people in the world today have sacrificed more to achieve it than the Hungarians.

I am not suggesting for one moment that Quebecers have suffered anything close to the terror inflicted upon Hungary by the Nazis or the Communists, in fact quite the opposite but what the Hungarian experienced clearly demonstrates is that there are many people in the world willing to risk everything, including their lives in order to achieve freedom and independence.

In an effort to be "masters in their own house" more than 300,000 Hungarians were exiled, imprisoned, tortured or killed.

Their fight for freedom and independence began on October 23, 1956 when more than 200,000 took to the streets of Budapest, tearing down red star signs, destroying Stalin's statue and taking over the state broadcast station. They appealed to the world for help but all that arrived were 30,000 Russian tanks.

More than 200,000 of the revolutionaries fled into Austria until their escape route was cut off. Thousands were killed. The U.S. called it a "monstrous crime" but along with the rest of the West did nothing.

Hungarians had to wait another 32 years under the Communist yoke before finally on the 24th of March 1990 free elections were held and Hungary at last was free and independent.

CHAPTER TEN

IS IT ONLY MONEY THAT KEEPS US TOGETHER?

Unlike the blood shed in Hungary and many other countries that have fought and attained independence over the years, not a single Quebecer would have to risk their life in order to achieve the independence so many of them say they long for. Even their risk of losing jobs would be minimal.

The only sacrifice Quebec would have to make would be to forfeit about eight billion dollars a year in transfer payments from the rest of Canada along with a few other perks such as thousands of cushy jobs in the federal public service. They might not have to give up their Canadian passports if they didn't choose to. I'll explain that in a later chapter.

Instead of draining the public purse with their yearly transfer payments, they could and surely would begin to extract some of the 46 billion barrels of oil and the trillions of cubic feet of natural gas that sit undisturbed beneath their soil and be far better off as an independent nation then they ever will be still sucking from the federal teat!

Could it be that the only thing that keeps Quebec in Canada are a few pieces of silver? Easy money!

There is certainly plenty of evidence that, if not entirely, it is mostly all about money. Were it not for the money the ROC pumps into Quebec every year from the equalization farce as well as the myriad of other grants, subsidies and benefits flowing from Ottawa, Quebec would have been gone long ago.

Time and time again Quebecers, or at least the majority of them, have demonstrated very clearly that they have a different view of Canada, and of the world than the rest of Canada. We've been taking separate paths for a long time and if we were brutally honest we'd all have to admit it.

The "two solitudes" have never been as divergent, as headed in separate directions, as they are today.

The farcical brief flare-up concerning turbanned soccer players is a typical example. Can you just imagine the uproar if any premier in the ROC publicly sided with a sports organization claiming that wearing turbans created a safety hazard to soccer players! It's not necessarily that one side is right and the other wrong. Not even a variation of that theme, it's just that we are different. Different language, different culture, different loyalties, different priorities, different view of the world and growing more different as the years progress. As further evidence of our differences, consider the uproar over Quebec's Charter of Values!

From participation in both World Wars, (opposed by most Quebecers) to the discriminatory provisions of Bill 101, to bilingualism, and multiculturalism (not accepted in Quebec), our Constitution, (not signed by Quebec) Quebec and the rest of Canada have been at constant loggerheads for much of our history.

Loggerheads which on December 21, 1989 led the Quebec National Assembly to employ the "Notwithstanding" Clause of the Charter of Rights and Freedoms in order to defy a Supreme Court ruling that Bill 101 contravened both Freedom of Expression and Equality Rights guaranteed in the Charter.

The Supreme Court ruled that Bill 101, known as the French Language Law, was unconstitutional. The law, greatly restricting English language rights was even criticized by the UN Human Rights Committee but was none-the-less passed by the Quebec National Assembly with the approval of the majority of Quebecers and has been subsequently amended seven times, each time to further restrict English language rights which are gradually becoming almost non-existent.

Today even the leader of the federal Liberal Party Justin Trudeau says he supports Bill 101 and no politician of any stripe dares suggest in public that it constitutes blatant discrimination against Anglos.

It is the only time the "Notwithstanding" clause has been used thus far in our history.

One more Quebec distinction!

CHAPTER ELEVEN

THE INFAMOUS BILL 101
(Charter of the French language)

Most Canadians have heard of Quebec's Bill 101. Few, including Quebec residents, understand how onerous and far reaching it is or how close it is to a unilateral declaration of independence. It is difficult to find any aspect of daily life in Quebec that is not affected by its provisions.

It is largely Bill 101 and its implementation that drove well over a quarter million Anglos and Allophones out of the province along with huge chunks of business and commerce.

Bill 101 is largely responsible for the Province's continual "have-not" status.

It is extremely difficult for reasonable people to read some of the key provisions of Bill 101 without asking these questions.

Why in the world did we stand by and let this happen? Why did the rest of Canada not tell Quebec when the Bill was first proposed that they had two choices?

Scrap the Bill as not only anti-democratic and a contravention of human rights, but totally unacceptable in a free society—or:

Face a Canada-wide referendum asking a simple question. Can Quebec remain within Confederation if Bill 101 becomes law?

Examine some of the key provisions of the Bill then ask yourself. If such a referendum on Quebec separation were held today, how would you vote? Should any jurisdiction that treats its minorities in such a disgraceful fashion be allowed to remain a part of Canada?

Containing more than 200 separate declarations and provisions, the Bill would occupy about 50 pages of this book if presented in its entirety but the following are some of the key declarations: (Accompanied occasionally by my observations in brackets).

PREAMBLE:

Whereas the French language, the distinctive language of a people that is in the majority French-speaking, is the instrument by which that people has articulated its identity:

Whereas the National Assembly of Quebec recognizes that Quebecers wish to see the quality and influence of the French language assured and is resolved therefore to make of French the language of Government and the Law, as well as the normal and everyday language of work, instruction, communication, commerce and business;

Whereas the National Assembly intends to pursue this objective in a spirit of fairness and open-mindedness, respectful of the institutions of the English-speaking community of Quebec and respectful of the ethnic minorities, whose valuable contribution to the development of Quebec it readily acknowledges;

Whereas the National Assembly of Quebec recognizes the right of the Amerinds and the Inuit of Quebec, the first inhabitants of this land, to preserve and develop their original language and culture;

Whereas these observations and intentions are in keeping with a new perception of the worth of national cultures in all parts of the earth, and of the obligation of every people to contribute in its special way to the international community;

Therefore, Her Majesty, with the advice and consent of the National Assembly of Quebec enacts as follows: (The "as follows" starts on the next page!)

(All of this sounds very reasonable but as someone once said the devil is in the details.)

One of the first acts of the Quebec Government utilizing Bill 101 was to inform all native Indians that if they wanted to continue their "privilege of English language schools", they would have to make an official, written request of the Government for the "right" to have their children taught in English. This created a huge uproar in many native communities.

"We were here first," said many of the Indian chiefs, "there is no damn way we are going, cap in hand, to anyone begging for anything, let alone a right we have had since Confederation, the right to educate our children in whatever language we choose!"

All hell broke loose!

Bridges, roads and in some cases entire native reserves were blockaded. Scattered incidents of violence threatened to escalate until large groups of Indian children attending English language high schools in the province simply walked out of class and established their own schools on their reserves.

My father was among those who led a large group of Indian children out of Billings High School in Chateauguay and helped to establish the highly successful "Kahnawake Survival School" on the nearby Kahnawake Mohawk reserve.

Since Native reserves are under federal jurisdiction there was nothing the Quebec government could do. Incidentally, the "Survival School" at Kahnawake continues to thrive and provide the kind of education that has helped to make that reserve's average income among the highest in the entire country.

As I've already pointed out, tens of thousands of other non-native Quebec residents, without the opportunity of establishing their own "survival schools", packed up their children, their possessions, their money and their businesses and left the province entirely!

Let's have a look at some of the things contained in Bill 101 that convinced so many non-Francophones to flee the province!

TITLE 1

STATUS OF THE FRENCH LANGUAGE

CHAPTER 1

THE OFFICIAL LANGUAGE OF QUEBEC

1. French is the official language of Quebec. (No cumbersome bilingualism *here!*)

CHAPTER 11

FUNDAMENTAL LANGUAGE RIGHTS

2. Every person has a right to have the civil administration, the health services and social services, the public utility enterprises, the professional orders, the associations of employees and all enterprises doing business in Quebec communicate with him in French. (No such right to communicate in English!)

3. In deliberative assembly, every person has a right to speak in French. (No problem until that right is expanded to the point where all public discourse, even in Anglo communities must be carried out in French!)

4. Workers have a right to carry on their activities in French. (Which means all levels of management must be French speaking!)

5. Consumers of goods and services have a right to be informed and served in French. (Hey, what about that bit about the right in the preamble for Natives to use their language? Essentially what this means is that even in the heart of an English speaking district no one gets a job unless they speak fluent French!)

6. Every person eligible for instruction in Quebec has a right to receive that instruction in French. (No such guarantee for those seeking instruction in English!)

CHAPTER III

THE LANGUAGE OF THE LEGISLATURE AND THE COURTS.

7. French is the language of the legislature and the courts in Quebec subject to the following:

(Here are whole series of provisions, all of which do provide some protection for those who speak only English. Section 4, for example states that either French or English may be used by any person in a Quebec court. The National Assembly recognized the fact that denying English language rights in the courts was a step too far).

CHAPTER IV

THE LANGUAGE OF THE CIVIL ADMINISTRATION

Once again here are a whole series of directives stating among other things that all government documents shall be in French only, except those dealing with governments outside Quebec. All notices of meetings, agendas and minutes must be draw up in French. Within government only French signs and posters will be allowed, other than those where reasons of health or public safety require the use of another language. This includes all traffic signs in the province. (This is really helpful for tourists trying to navigate around the province.)

Section 20 of this chapter states: **In order to be appointed, transferred or promoted to an office in the civil administration, a knowledge of the official language (French) appropriate to the office applied for is required. In this regard the "Office Québécois de la langue francais"** (the language police) **will rule on what constitutes what is an appropriate level of French required.**

(This undoubtedly accounts for the fact that while Anglos comprise more than 7% of Quebec's population they hold fewer than 3% of the Provincial public service jobs.)

SECTION 29.1— DANGER!

No provision of Bill 101 poses more of a threat to minority rights than section 29.1 of chapter IV.

It states as follows:

29.1 English language school boards and the Commission scolaire de Littoral (private school company) **are recognized school bodies that the Office** (the language police) **shall recognize at the request of the municipality, body or institution:**

A municipality of which more than half the residents have English as their mother tongue.

A body under the authority of one or more municipalities that participates in the administration of their territory, where each such municipality is a recognized municipality or

A health and social services institution listed in the Schedule where it provides services to persons who, in the majority speak a language other than French.

The Government may, at the request of a body or institution that no longer satisfies the condition, which enabled it to obtain the recognition of the Office, withdraw such recognition if it considers it appropriate in the circumstance and after having consulted the Office. Such a request shall be made to the Office, which shall transmit it to Government with a copy of the record. The Government shall inform the Office and the body or institution of its decision.

(Simply stated what it means is that if a municipality or district does not have an English speaking majority they have no right to an English language school board or hospital board. As the Anglo population continues to decline this means fewer and fewer English language schools and medical facilities.)

There is no question that since the passage of Bill 101 there have been English language schools and school boards in areas where Anglos are not in the majority, but with Pauline Marois and her government at the helm it has become obvious that there will be a major clampdown and Bill 101 provisions concerning school and hospital boards will be strictly enforced.

There is some speculation that if the trend continues it will soon be virtually impossible to obtain an education in English anywhere in the province.

If Bill 14 is passed it will make 155 amendments to Bill 101, further drastically reducing minority rights in Quebec. As I write this it appears that Ms. Marois may not have sufficient support in the legislature to get all of this new attack on English speakers through the legislature but even if not passed in its entirety, it is as Barbara Kay recently wrote in the National Post a "pathological attack on the sin of speaking English" and serves one more notice to Anglos that they are not welcome in Quebec by large numbers of its citizens.

(I will deal with the implications of Bill 14 in a later chapter.)

Before we get back to the provisions of Bill 101—let's have a look, through one man's eyes at the consequences of another one of the bill's draconian provisions.

I refer here to Section 35, dealing with the language of semi-public agencies.

CHAPTER TWELVE

NOT WANTED!

One of those driven out of Quebec by Section 35 of Bill 101 is a psychiatrist named James Ross, of London, ON, whose essay appeared in the April 2, 2013 edition of the Globe and Mail.

Dr. Ross first explains how, as a new graduate in psychiatry, he decided to establish a practice in Montreal. He relates how hard he worked to learn French then writes:

"I thought I had found my French groove. Near the end of my residency, a temporary staff position in Quebec's Kafkaesque health system appeared possible.

People warned me about the exam administered by l'Office Quebecois de la langue francais. Doctors must pass it within four years to keep their license in Quebec. Many of my "Rest of Canada" colleagues had failed it several times. Anglophones from Quebec, some of whom do not speak French well, are not subjected to the exam.

I hoped that my dedication to learning French day to day would pay off. Being very busy with the transition from residency to practice, I put off taking the exam. My training complete, I received a 'permis temporaire' to practice psychiatry."

He then goes on to explain what happened when he finally did show up to write his exam:

"Finally someone arrived to guide us to the exam room where we all wrote disarmingly simple (grade 6-level) tests of French comprehension. I aced that part.

Then came written expression. I was instructed to answer a very confusing question. How would I justify to office staff the need for a new technology, to which they were resistant?

Without context and a clear reason why these generic employees should adopt some amorphous form of technology, writing an answer would be confusing in any language. I came up with a weak rationale in the best francais I could muster.

Afterward I was guided to a small room where a seemingly pleasant man asked me to explain in French what I did in my job. He stared at me while I spoke nervously. I learned later that 5 percent is deducted for every grammatical error.

When I called in to discuss my marks (20 per cent on written expression and 40 per cent on oral expression, though I did pass the comprehension), the examiner explained that while there were clearly no problems in my ability to communicate, I had made grammatical errors in the gender agreement of adjectives and nouns and used far too many 'Anglicism's'—words that are used by Francophones but considered too English to be acceptable in civilized speech."

Dr. Ross then goes on to explain how over the next two years he took more French classes, tried yet another French exam and failed it then finally, in frustration, he writes:

Mastering French grammar on top of a full caseload and clinical teaching proved beyond me.

It ate away at me when people who had spoken French from birth or were not at the mercy of the OQLF to keep their jobs, made remarks about my limited language ability even though I treated many psychiatric patients in French.

I found a job opportunity in Ontario, where I could get a license free of shame and funding to improve my qualifications as a medical teacher rather than a French grammar ace."

James Ross fell afoul of Section 35 of Bill 101 that states the following:

The professional orders shall not issue permits except to persons whose knowledge of the official language is appropriate to the practice of their profession.

A person is deemed to have the appropriate knowledge if:

He has received, full time, no less than three years of secondary or post-secondary instruction provided in French.

He has passed the fourth or fifth year secondary level examinations in French as the first language.

From and after the school year 1985-86 he obtains a secondary school certificate in Quebec.

In all other cases, a person must obtain a certificate issued by the Office Quebecois de la langue francais or hold a certificate defined as equivalent by regulation of the Government.

The Government by regulation may determine the procedure and conditions of issue of certificates by the Office, establish the rules governing composition of an examining committee to be formed by the Office, provide for the mode of operation of that committee and determine criteria for evaluating the appropriate knowledge of French for the practice of a profession or a category of professions and a made of evaluating such knowledge

Interpretation, as James Ross discovered, good luck finding work in any of the professions in Quebec unless you have graduated from a

French high school or university or a Quebec English high school after the 1985-86 school year. In other words says La Belle Province—we don't want any upstart doctors, lawyers, dentists, teachers, nurses, social workers, etc. crossing from foreign territory in the ROC or elsewhere, into our little preserve!

Now mind you, any attempt to stop Quebec professionals or trades people from working wherever they like in the rest of Canada, no matter how well they speak any language, would be greeted with howls of protest.

Just ask us here in Ottawa!

Some mornings, cars or trucks bearing Ontario license plates look like proverbial lonely little petunias in a sea of Quebec plates flooding the parking lots of various building projects. Finding an Ontario vehicle in the parking lot of some of our east end hospitals is virtually impossible.

And don't even ask how many Quebec patients are occupying Ontario hospital beds. You really don't want to know! It will just drive you crazy, especially when you realize how badly the Quebec government shortchanges Ontario hospitals and in the process fleeces Ontario taxpayers.

I've never been able to obtain accurate numbers, but as best I can determine, on average, an Ontario hospital receives about 20 per cent less per procedure or stay in bed for a Quebec patient than it does from OHIP for an Ontario patient. To put it in simpler terms. If OHIP pays, lets say, the Queensway Carleton Hospital a thousand dollars to remove an Ontario appendix, The Quebec government will only pay an Ontario hospital $800 for exactly the same removal of a Quebec appendix!

With that kind of a sweetheart deal, why would Quebec bother building new hospitals anywhere within easy driving range of Ontario?

The easy answer is they don't!

CHAPTER THIRTEEN

THEY GOT ME!

CHAPTER VII BILL 101

The Language of Commerce and Business.

I got caught red-handed by this dandy little chapter. It cost me a bundle! By no means was I alone. This is the chapter of Bill 101 that saw hundreds, if not thousands of business people driven either half crazy or right out of the Province. My story is only too typical.

In 1978, three partners and I founded Ottawa Travel, which after we bought Algonquin Travel, became the largest independent travel agency in Ontario. At my urging (sorry about that) we located several branches in Quebec. Big mistake!

It was just about then that the "tongue troopers" descended upon anything that even looked or smelled English and ordered it destroyed. The problem was that on the Quebec side our big (and very expensive) neon signs stated proudly in large lighted individual letters VOYAGES OTTAWA TRAVEL.

"The word travel is unacceptable," we were told in no uncertain terms. "You've got 30 days to take it down or we close you down!"

Removing the offending word was no small task, requiring the services of an electrician, a technician and a small crane. You can imagine the expense!

Problem was, even after the offensive word had been removed, if you looked closely you could see where the letters T R A V E L had been fastened to the bulkhead of the offices. "Oh well, I said to myself, "It looks kind of silly but at least I got the law off my back!"

Wrong!

This ghostly vestige of the iniquitous word drove the tongue troopers nuts! They took it as a personal insult. I'm sure they were convinced I was doing this with the deliberate intent of embarrassing every decent Quebecer.

Without further notice they descended on all three of our Quebec branches and threatened to evacuate our employees and padlock the doors. It took all of my powers of persuasion to convince them that my failing eyesight was such that I hadn't noticed the problem but was very sorry for the error of my ways and would try to do better.

Actually I think it was the fortuitous arrival of my very attractive French Canadian wife (at the time) that did the trick but that's another story.

I was given five days to once and for all get my act together and properly eradicate the offending word or it was the end of Voyages Ottawa with or without the Travel.

Under the circumstances I did the only thing I could.

The paint I used didn't quite match anything in the entire building. I'm a terrible painter at the best of times and in anger am rivaled by a three year old.

When finished, what used to be a very attractive sign now looked a mess, and remained that way for years, but at least we were legal.

A brave victory for Chapter VII of Bill 101! Another attack on the French language thwarted!

Actually Chapter VII—the Language of Commerce and Business costs all of us Canadians a good chunk of money since among other things it dictates that the labels of every product sold in Quebec including any warranty and or instructions must be in French. Since these products are sold outside Quebec they must of course also include English. The actual cost of bilingualism on every product sold in Canada has never been even estimated to my knowledge but you can be sure it's not cheap.

This is also the chapter that dictates:

52.1 All computer software, including game software and operating systems, whether installed or uninstalled must be available in French unless no French version exists.

54. Toys and games, except those referred to in Section 52.1 which require the use of a non-French vocabulary for their operation are prohibited on the Quebec market, unless a French version of the toy or game is available on the Quebec market on no less favorable terms.

In carefully examining all clauses of Bill 101, I am convinced that VOYAGES OTTAWA TRAVEL was guilty of breaking not one, but probably three separate laws.

Section 58 for example states: **Public signs and posters and commercial advertising must be in French. They may also be both in French and another language provided that French is markedly predominant. However,** (this is where I think they got me) **the Government may determine, by regulation, the places, cases, conditions or circumstances where public signs and posters and commercial advertising must be in French only.**

Then further along is section 64, which states: **to obtain juridicial personality, it is necessary to have a name in French.**

And Section 65, which states: **Every name that is not in French must be changed before December 31, 1980, unless the Act under which the enterprise is incorporated does not allow it.**

(So is that two or three laws Voyages Ottawa Travel broke?)

In thinking about it today I suppose I should thank my lucky stars that they didn't rule that the word Ottawa had to be removed as well!

CHAPTER FOURTEEN

THE EXODUS CLAUSE!

Chapter VIII BILL 101

The Language of Instruction

Section 73 of this chapter is perhaps the most discriminatory of all and has undoubtedly caused more outright hardship and ill will than any other provision of Bill 101.

It states as follows:

The following children, at the request of one of their parents may receive instruction in English:

(1) a child whose father or mother is a Canadian citizen and received elementary instruction in English in Canada, provided that that instruction constitutes the major part of the elementary instruction he or she received in Canada

(2) a child whose father or mother is a Canadian citizen and who has received or is receiving elementary or secondary instruction in English in Canada and the brothers and sisters of that child, provided

that the instruction constitutes the major part of the elementary or secondary instruction received by the child in Canada.

Let's think about all those children who are thus denied the right to an English language education in Quebec.

The children of immigrants not yet Canadian citizens.

The children of parents educated in a country other than Canada.

The children of parents educated in any language other than English.

The children of non-Canadians temporarily living or working in Quebec

(Except under some conditions members of the military)

(5) The children of English speaking parents who received the bulk of their education in French. (French immersion).

Then there is a dandy little restriction in section 84 of Chapter VIII

Which states:

No secondary school leaving certificate may be issued to a student who does not have the speaking and writing knowledge of French required by the curricula of the Ministere de Education, du Loisir et du Sport!

Imagine the plight of the poor kid from Calgary whose parents moved him to Quebec during his last two years of high school. Think he'll ever be able to learn enough French to pass the French language test?

In order to obtain a high school diploma he or she will obviously have to leave Quebec at least for that final year.

In fairness, some special concessions have been made for some native Indian groups, in particular the Cree of northern Quebec.

If you still don't believe that Quebec has long been marching off in a different direction than the rest of Canada, a kind of de facto independence, consider how many residents and businesses the following chapter has driven out of the province.

CHAPTER FIFTEEN

THE GET YOUR BUSINESS OUT OF HERE CLAUSE!

CHAPTER V (I have no idea why these chapters are not in sequence in Bill 101, but they are not)

Francization of Enterprises

135. This chapter applies to all enterprises, including public utility enterprises.

136. Enterprises employing 100 or more persons must form a francization committee composed of six or more persons.

This francization committee shall analyze the language situation in the enterprise and make a report to the management of the enterprise for transmission to the Office. Where necessary, the committee shall devise a francization program for the enterprise and supervise its implementation. Where a francization certificate is issued to the enterprise, the committee shall ensure that the use of French remains generalized at all levels of the enterprise according to the terms of section 141.

Several sections that follow specify how this francization committee shall be formed and how frequently it must meet.

139. An enterprise which employees 50 or more persons for more than a period of six months must register with the Office within six months of the end of that period. For that purpose the enterprise shall inform the Office of the number of persons it employs and provide it with general information on its legal status and its functional structure and on the nature of its activities.

140. If the Office considers, after examining the analysis of the enterprise's linguistic situation, that the use of French is generalized at all levels of the enterprise according to the terms of section 141, it shall issue a francization certificate.

If however the Office considers that the use of French is not generalized at all levels of the enterprise, it shall notify the enterprise that it must adopt a francization program.

141. The francization program is intended to generalize the use of French at all levels of the enterprise through:

The knowledge of the official language on the part of management, the members of the professional orders and the other members of the personnel.

An increase, where necessary at all levels of the enterprise, including the board of directors, in the number of persons having a good knowledge of the French language so as to generalize its use.

The use of French as the language of work and as the language of internal communication.

The use of French in the working documents of the enterprise, especially in manuals and catalogues.

The use of French in communications with the civil administration, clients, suppliers, the public and shareholders, except in the latter case if the enterprise is a closed company within the mean of the Securities Act (chapterV-1.1)

The use of French terminology
The use of French in public signs and posters and commercial advertising.

Appropriate policies for hiring, promotion and transfer.
The use of French in information technologies.

Essentially Bill 101 states that only those who speak French fluently can work in any Quebec enterprise with 50 or more employees A few concessions are allowed in the case of an employee nearing retirement or when a head office of a foreign company is involved.

CHAPTER SIXTEEN

THE TONGUE TROOPERS!

I have several correspondents from business owners and managers who say the francization committees are almost always comprised entirely of language zealots who make life hell for them.

A former Macdonald College classmate tells me that he was "reported" to the dreaded "tongue troopers" once for putting up some posters in his office using the words "hot dogs" and "hamburgers."

What really upset him was the fact that the posters were for a company picnic during which free hotdogs and hamburgers were being handed out!

"Three little 'Napoleons' from the 'Office' appeared on the scene," he says, "and in front of all our employees lectured management on the horrors of using English words in the workplace. It was like a scene right out of Kafka!"

Actually my old college buddy got off relatively easy.

The punishment for language blasphemy is about as severe as those doled out these days for holding up a bank or shooting your boss!

Fines for an individual caught breaking the law by using an English word, range from $600 to $6,000 for the first offence. Fines are doubled for the second offence. In the case of an enterprise of any size the fine is from $1,500 to $20,000, doubled for the second offence. And not only that—if the "Office" decides that you made some money by the unlawful use of an English word the profit and a further fine of an undetermined amount will be tacked onto the first fine!

God help you if you try to get of the tongue troops any kind of lip. You are at their mercy and they have almost unlimited powers.

And as you might expect with this kind of draconian edict, once you are charged you are presumed guilty. The burden of proof of innocence lies with the individual or enterprise that has been charged.

If this doesn't sound very Canadian you are correct. This kind of fascism is only found in Quebec! Don't forget Bill 101 was found to be unconstitutional by the Supreme Court. The Human Rights Commission of the United Nations ruled that Bill 101 contravened human rights.

The Charter of the French Language (La charte de la langue francais (Bill 101) was proposed by Camille Laurin, Minister of Cultural Development in the first Parti Quebecois government of Premier Rene Levesque. It was passed by the National Assembly and became law on August 26,1977. The bill has been amended and strengthened at least seven times since then, each time creating great controversy and passionate debate in Quebec and across the Country.

Let's have a look at some of the things we can thank Bill 101 for.

According to Statistics Canada between 1971 and 2006 a total of 284,000 English-speaking Quebecers fled Quebec, mostly for other parts of Canada. In addition, another 82,000 Allophones (non French or English mother tongue) left the province. Between 1976 and 1981 a total of 106,300 Anglos packed up Uhauls and headed down highway 401 for friendlier territory.

Is it the largest peacetime exodus of any ethnic group from any jurisdiction in the Western world since the Second World War! Not a pretty picture is it?

In 2001, those claiming English as their mother tongue comprised 10.5% of Quebec's total population. Ten years later in 2011 that had fallen to only 7.7%.

All of this provides powerful backing to my contention that now is the perfect time to wave a friendly goodbye to Quebec.

Explain yourself you say!

Gladly.

When The Parti Quebecois was first elected with Rene Levesque at its head there was panic across the land. Many of you will recall that famous Montreal Gazette cartoon featuring a chain smoking Levesque admonishing us all to, "Take a valium".

Levesque's election launched the great Anglo exodus from Quebec but what really ignited the "let's get the hell out of here" tidal wave of escapers was Bill 101.

Many of those, who for one reason or another, chose to remain in the province, did their best to raise bloody hell. Protests broke out each time a new language restriction was imposed. They marched in the streets. Appeals were made to the rest of Canada to come to the rescue of oppressed Anglos.

English language rights organizations sprang up across the province and recruited tens of thousands. A small town undertaker took the matter to the United Nations. English dominated parts of the province threatened to secede. Police who feared violence from pitchfork bearing outraged Shawvillians (residents of Shawville) stopped a merry band of "tongue troopers" heading into the Pontiac, where a rogue English sign had been spotted in a store window.

Angry phone calls to my radio talk show in Ottawa poured in from anguished Anglos from as far away as the Eastern Townships. Depending upon their frustration level and temperament, most of them were either demanding or begging the Federal Government to do something to stop the blatant discrimination. On more than one occasion the call was from someone who had already fled Quebec or was in the process of packing up.

In the midst of the "great exodus" I hosted a talk show at CFRB Radio in Toronto, and asked listeners to tell me why they had left and what they missed most about Montreal. For two solid hours the phone lines were jammed with callers who talked about the memories they had of life in Quebec.

They talked longingly of the good times strolling along Ste. Catherine Street, which even in the small wee hours of the morning, was always jumping with people. They said they missed the excitement of Canadiens games at the Forum, Gibby's Steakhouse, the bar at Chateau Champlain, the lookout atop Mt. Royal. Almost all recalled the glorious days of Expo 67 and with a few chuckles, adventures at the Big "O" with the Expos and the Alouettes. A couple callers spoke fondly of afternoons spent in Wanda's, a famous Montreal strip bar.

I remember, in particular, one caller who talked very eloquently about what a joy it was to live and work in the high octane atmosphere of two languages and two cultures working together, enjoying each other, creating in Montreal one of the world's most vibrant, exciting and interesting cities. "Just to feel the energy, the sexual tension, hear the laughter and the buzz as you patrolled along Crescent Street on a Friday night was a lot more fun than anything we experience even today in Toronto," he claimed.

He paused for a moment. "Well that's the way it used to be. When our family left in 1990, driven out actually, Montreal was no longer a fun place for anyone, especially for Anglos like us. At least a quarter of the stores along Ste. Catherine, were boarded up. There were empty office buildings everywhere; some of the finest restaurants had already closed. There were still crowds along Crescent Street, but the fun had gone out of it.

It got so bad that my wife and I were afraid to be overheard speaking English in public. Chances were if someone didn't snarl at you, you'd rate a nasty look or two. Even in downtown Montreal, which always used to be so cosmopolitan, you just didn't feel comfortable as an English speaking resident.

My company moved its head office here to Toronto," he said wistfully, "but my wife had already made up our minds that Quebec didn't want us anymore strictly because of the language we spoke and it was time to move out. The final straw was the fact that since my wife was born and raised in Ireland, and I came to Canada from the United States it meant that we didn't have a legal right to send our children to an English school, even though we were both Canadian citizens. This we found outrageous. As you know, we are not the only ones. Almost all of my co-workers and a good many of our friends made the same decision or had already left.

One of the saddest aspects about all of this", he told me "is that I cannot recall a single Francophone, including some with whom we were friends, expressing any remorse for what was happening. In fact you got the idea that most of them were saying silently to themselves, good riddance. I hope I am wrong about that but I suspect I am not."

He and other callers talked a good deal about some of their favourite haunts in Montreal, several mentioned that the thing they missed the most was the St. Patrick's Day Parade.

When I suggested that there was nothing stopping anyone from going back to Montreal to take in the parade or a Canadiens game the typical answer was expressed by one very adamant woman who said something to the effect: "No way, they forced me out, they made it clear I wasn't wanted because I spoke English, I will never spend another cent in that damned province."

She was angry, but most callers were more sad than mad. But when asked most of the callers maintained they didn't want Quebec to separate. Many expressed the hope that Quebecers would, as one caller said, "come to their senses, stop the nonsense and get back to normal and be Canadian again!"

That was 1993.

Twenty years ago people still cared. Even those who felt they had been driven out were not prepared to say goodbye to Quebec. They, along with most of us, really believed that the good nature and the sense of fairness of the average Quebecer would come floating to the surface, the zealots would be silenced and Quebec would once again take her place as the great, open, cosmopolitan, province that opened her arms and joyously welcomed the world to Expo 67 and the 1976 Olympics.

That was then! This is now!

A totally different story today. A totally different attitude, both outside Quebec and within her borders.

Today, only the terminally naive or the odd stray Martian could possibly believe that things are going to improve for Anglos in Quebec, or that there is any widespread desire on behalf of the average Quebecer to embrace Canada or Canadian values. Canadian money perhaps!

More to the point—today hardly anyone cares.

It's true outside Quebec in the rest of Canada.

It's true inside Quebec, even within the tiny English-speaking minority, which for want of a better label I am calling "the lamb lobby"! A tiny minority either so dispirited or perhaps so well integrated into Quebec society that they can barely muster a weak peep of protest over the gravest of indignities.

I say it again. Now is the perfect time to wave a friendly goodbye to Quebec. The affection on both sides has been replaced by apathy. Today we barely tolerate each other.

Just as with a married couple that has lost interest in each other, a parting of the ways now would be a relatively painless affair. A Czech Republic and Slovakia kind of velvet divorce!

When the passion is no long aflame the will to fight flickers out.

With its huge oil and gas reserves, Quebec has the potential to be totally self sufficient, in fact it would probably be compelled to become vastly better off than it is today within Confederation.

The rest of Canada would be relieved, not only of the tremendous financial and political burden of Quebec, but a major portion of the country's bilingualism bill. You can imagine the savings!

CHAPTER SEVENTEEN

A CYNICAL ASSAULT ON ANGLO RIGHTS!

Never was the need for us to go our separate ways more evident than when Pauline Marois introduced Bill 14 which is, as the National Post said on April 6, 2013 **"A Cynical Assault on Anglo Rights"**.

This is a bill, which if passed would among other things:

(1) rescind a regulation permitting English-speaking members of the Canadian Armed Forces who are temporarily stationed in Quebec to have their children schooled in English, thus forcing the closure of several of the few remaining English schools in the province.

(2) officially bilingual municipalities would lose their bilingual status if the English language population fell below 50%, which today means even such western Quebec communities as Chelsea would not be allowed to communicate with any of their residents in a language other than French.

(3) an employee required to communicate in a language other than French would have the right to sue his or her employer for monetary damages.

(4) all daycares would have to provide French language instruction, essentially forcing the closure of thousands of informal daycare facilities. There is some question whether daycare provided by relatives, including grandparents might have to adhere to this requirement!

(5) prevent businesses with more than 25 employees from using English in the workplace.

(6) introduce a mandatory French proficiency test for all Quebec high school and CEGEP graduates.

(7) make it harder for the 24 per cent of non-French speaking immigrants who come to Quebec annually to find work in small businesses.

(8) according to the McGill Daily newspaper: " *Bill 14 employs an underhanded method to revoke citizens' right to access government documents in English.*

"Under the new piece of legislation," states the paper, *"the city of Cote-Saint-Luc, for example, could potentially lose its bilingual status because a large percentage of the population identifies themselves as neither French nor English. Citizens who don't identify as having English as their mother tongue—for example those who consider Yiddish or Italian as their mother tongue, but who use English regularly—would therefore lose their ability to access municipal documents in English, as they would only be published in French."*

It is unclear exactly how such a measure would protect French, but it's clear how it would make life more difficult for Anglophones."

The McGill Daily goes on to say, *"For many English-speaking Quebec residents, however, the extension of the language laws in Bill 14 disrupts the status quo between the government and the Anglophone population.*

The Anglophone community largely accepts that French proficiency is necessary to obtain employment in Quebec, and the tacit compromise vis-à-vis Bill 101 has lasted without challenge for longer than a decade.

Anglophones have their current rights in return for assenting to the bill's provisions. In face of this new development, a sense of anxiety among English speakers is palpable, as 42 per cent of respondents in a recent poll of Anglophone Quebec residents said they are considering leaving the province."

The Globe and Mail in a March 1, 2013 editorial stated, " *The Parti Québécois minority government is currently promoting Bill 14, a massive revision and expansion of every section of Quebec's Charter of the French Language, as well as of the Quebec Charter of Human Rights and Freedoms, which was tabled in December. Bill 14, if passed as introduced, will give dramatic new powers to language inspectors, to the government and to hard-line language activists looking to make hay."*

The Globe goes on to say, *"Take the dreaded language inspectors, for instance. Under the section of the Charter of French Language governing the OQFL as it currently stands, inspectors can 'request' documents from people or businesses suspected of language violations. Under the amendments proposed in Bill 14, inspectors will have the power to 'require the production of any book, account, record, file or other document for examination or for the purpose of making copies of extracts,' and to 'seize any thing which he or she believes on reasonable grounds may prove the commission of an offence.'"*

These are policing powers, not powers of inspection.

As well, where currently someone alleged to have committed an infraction is given time to comply before charges are laid, Bill 14 removes the mention of a compliance period. Instead, once an infraction is suspected, the OQFL "shall refer the matter to the Director of Criminal and Penal Prosecutions so that appropriate penal proceedings may be instituted."

~ • ~

Please understand. This is not North Korea we're talking about. This is all happening in Canada!

As my favourite uncle used to say—"How do you like them apples eh?"

Bill 14 proposes many other odious yokes to be placed upon the shoulders of those unfortunate enough to have been born into an English speaking family, but we have all become so used to this kind of pathological fear and hatred of the English language that it's being met for the most part with a very dull ho-hum!

CHAPTER EIGHTEEN

MOVE ACROSS THE RIVER!

When dealing with numbers and broad concepts such as government bills we sometimes tend to forget that it's real people involved. The following email is one of the most poignant and the most revealing that I have received. You can sense the frustration, the anger, the disappointment and yes the sadness that in many ways reflect the sentiments of many of us—on both sides of the Ottawa River.

Morning Lowell.

Originally penned this to send as a letter to an editor and may still do so if parts of Bill 14 make it into law. We're a family born and bred in the Pontiac area.

As a parent of a couple children that are coming of age, my thoughts sometimes turn to what key pieces of direction I can give them as they head into adulthood. Most of us are familiar with the conversation. The one where parents help their children break with the past to achieve a better future.

As a child my plea was for higher education, so I could get a good job and have a prosperous future. Good advice indeed for someone from a small town in the Pontiac. Not that small town traditions are anything less. Hard work anywhere is invaluable. Higher education just allows for more prosperity and security with the same amount of work.

This has become a given nowadays. My children will both pursue post secondary education because it's expected. My wife and I will save to help them achieve their goal, given our family's heritage and values.

But now comes the question, what advice can I impart that will improve my children's lives in the most basic of ways? As my thoughts turn to this, one bit of counsel I really feel I can give them that will better their lives is simple—leave Quebec.

Yes a rather startling conclusion I must admit. We're multi-generational Quebecers going back to when Europeans hopped off a boat here. A mix of Native, French, Anglo backgrounds. I'm proud to be from the Pontiac. There's a wealth of genuinely nice people in the area. A seemingly rare utopia in Quebec where people of all stripes, for the most part, simply get along.

The sad reality however is that it's becoming increasingly difficult to live with the parameters of our family values in this province.

My wife and I are both fluently bilingual and we've made the best efforts to provide the same advantages to our children. We encourage the use of French to communicate outside of our home and we preach tolerance.

We also like to live in a world of hope. The hope here is that everybody makes an effort to meet in the middle, that all Quebecers and Canadians from the rest of the country can unit to create a place to live where everyone can flourish.

The stark truth of our circumstance however, is that rights for Anglophones and Allophones have been progressively stripped away for decades now. Essential rights and freedoms—communication, representation, education, equality. The same rights that our grandfathers went to war in Europe to defend, many with their lives. Rights that are regularly surrendered to the French majority with so little thought to the faceless people (to them) that they affect.

It hasn't been a full frontal assault, but a systematic chipping away. Each one offered as a consensus choice. "The least we can do to protect French culture against the hordes of Anglophones banging at the gate," is their message. They seem oblivious to the fact that no one is at the gate anymore. No one I know outside the Province wants to move here anymore and it has nothing to do with a willingness to speak French.

There's no white knight coming to our rescue in Quebec. The Federal Government has exemplified Pontius Pilate and effectively washed its hands of the fate of the minorities in our province. It's all wrapped up in the guise of words like jurisdiction and asymmetrical federalism. Greed and apathy are what it really is. The torch handed to them from failing hands was sold off for a shot at an easy re-election and a cushy pension.

I ask myself how can I espouse a system where an elderly woman that decides to move closer to her children in her elder years can't go to the hospital alone because it will be illegal for the staff to speak to her in her language? A system where an elderly man won't understand the notice he receives that his taxes are in arrears? A system where an Anglophone child with difficulties learning French will never have a shot at getting a job? A system where a person of any heritage that decides to school their children wholly in French loses further rights to an English education?

The answer is I cannot support or espouse such a system.

And I ask, how can many of my Francophone neighbours continue to support politicians that would strip human rights by labelling us "cultural communities" instead of "ethnic minorities"? Remove our ability to run for office if we don't pass a French exam. Remove English words from a restaurant or hospital. Squeeze English school boards to the point where they must close.

What ransoms are Francophones willing to pay from their collective conscience to ensure English words need not be spoken or heard? These are rights Francophones are losing as well!

There are a few fools on both sides that would incite rather than collaborate. These people shouldn't have been allowed to drive the agenda for the future.

For those of us who live here, this is our fight because we already have so much invested, but the fight doesn't have to belong to my children. The price we must pay to become accepted as true Quebecers will never be high enough. The price we pay to stay here is already too much.

So I am left with this. I must tell my kids to move across the river and enjoy their freedoms until Quebec becomes the place it should be and we all hope it someday will be!

Guy Petrin, Luskville, PQ

~ • ~

CHAPTER NINETEEN

DRIVEN OUT!

More than 300,000 Anglophones and Allophones fled Quebec following the FLQ crisis and Bill 101. There are more than 300,000 stories. This is just one of them:

Lowell, you ask for stories of those of us who had to leave Quebec because of its racist policies. This is not my story, but rather that of my father.

In 1954 my father arrived in Montreal from Italy with not much more than the clothes on his back, and a heart full of hope. A distant cousin employed him as a dishwasher in a little restaurant on Ste. Hubert near Jean Talon. Actually employed is too generous a word. My father for the first three years in Canada was essentially a slave, working for slave wages and sleeping on a basement floor.

But as with many of his background and generation, he managed to save a few dollars and in 1962 opened a little pizza parlour called " A———'s in the heart of Montreal's Little Italy on Jean Talon.

Move forward 20 some odd years and my father is now proud "Papa" to me and my sister—supported now by a much larger Italian Restaurant—whose name my mother doesn't want published for fear of retaliation.

His first problem was with a gang of small time thugs who demanded what they called protection money. When he threw them out of his restaurant he was threatened and several nights later some kind of explosive was set off in the alley at the side of his building. No damage was done, but some customers were frightened off. This kind of harassment continued for the better part of a year but when police were notified they simply laughed at my father and believe it or not had the nerve to suggest that it might be a good idea to slip a couple of the "cops on the beat" a few bucks so they would pay closer attention. You've got to understand that at that time the Italians and French Canadians in the area were constantly feuding. They hated each other and most of the police were French.

The real trouble however began when Quebec's famous "tongue troopers" began harassing him. He had to change his store sign to remove several English words—all his menus had to be re-done— and most of the signage inside. Then they set up some kind of French language committee in his restaurant and he was fined, according to him at least six or seven times—the last time the fine was in excess of two thousand dollars—he still isn't sure what he did wrong.

Then he ran into trouble with the Liquor Control Board of Quebec (or whatever they call it there) once again it had something to do with not speaking to customers first in French. Inspectors would call his restaurant to make a reservation and if they were not addressed first in French—more fines—until finally they took away his liquor license for three months.

Whether this is true I cannot say, but my father became convinced that most of his troubles were being spurred on by two French Canadians who had opened a new Italian Restaurant just around the block on Ste. Hubert.

He made the mistake of suggesting this to a government official and before you knew it there were threats of slander and more harassment from the "tongue troopers" and the liquor board.

Frustrated beyond belief and nearly out of his head with worry, he finally sold his business for what was obviously far below its value. He moved all of us to Montreal West then as the government came after him for what they claimed was an unpaid fine plus interest he left the province in disgust and with his heart broken. He died in Toronto two years ago, far too young. My mother still lives there.

I am sure my father's story—in fact our family's story— is not that different from the stories of thousands of others essentially driven out of a part of Canada for no reason other than our race!

J.T. Anderson, Brampton, ON

~ • ~

Here's another exodus story:

I have many fond memories of Montreal and the area. My first husband and I moved to Dorval shortly after we graduated from Queen's University in 1969. As an electrical engineer, Wayne was offered a job with Northern Electric. I went to work with Texas Instruments. It was a great life for a newly married young couple. Language was not a problem. Most of our neighbours were English speaking and we quickly made friends.

Life in Quebec in the late 60's and early 70's was exciting; we both did our best to acquire something more than our high school French. We didn't have a whole lot of money in those early days, what young couple does, but you could spend an entire afternoon—most of a day in fact— just wandering around Ste. Catherine St. or Old Montreal without spending anything more than the price of a couple coffees.

Sadly the good life didn't last nearly long enough. The FLQ crisis, the growing separatist agitation, the increasing hostile environment for Anglophones began to take its toll. We began to attend farewell parties for some of our friends and neighbours who had decided to head for more friendly territory or more frequently whose companies pulled up stakes and left Quebec.

It was only a matter of time until we suffered the same fate. In 1972 Northern Electric announced it was moving its Quebec operations (or at least most of them) to Brampton and those employees who chose to follow them were more than welcome to do so.

We really had no choice. Sadly we left Quebec, moved to Orangeville, raised a family, moved to Ottawa and the rest as they say is history!

Deborah Dean

Author's note: I'm glad the way things turned out, since Deborah and I have been together now for nearly 33 years!

~ • ~

And then there is this story:

You were asking about our Quebec experience and exodus. Here is ours:

Both my wife and I were born and educated in Montreal, Ville St. Laurent in fact. I'm now 62, Nancy is 60 and we are happily living in Delta, BC. I'm Scottish descent and Nancy is Irish—we're tagged Anglos!

During my employment at the HQ of the Bank of Montreal on what was St. James Street in Old Montreal, between the years of 1973 and 1977, it became clear that if I was to advance my career it was not going to happen in Quebec due to me being an Anglo. It is important to note that the ability to speak French didn't matter, what became to matter was our heritage—whether we were French Canadian or not. We were fully aware, as we are today, that the level of overt racism and or discrimination against people—founding people such as ourselves or families such as ours, had become a way of life that was accepted and implemented by officialdom at the provincial and even the federal level.

At that time it was also becoming very clear, due to rumours running through the Bank during the winter of 75/76 that the head office was relocating out of Quebec to Toronto. This together with all the other major banks and head offices of corporations too numerous to mention. My wife and I had several discussions concerning relocation to Toronto but that was just not how we envisioned our future unfolding.

However, during the summer and fall of 1976, we made a decision to cut our umbilical cord and head to the West Coast. We moved out in the summer of 1977 and over the following few years everyone else in our family left Quebec as well. I can't overstate what a profound decision this was that we made together as young adults.

It meant that as newly weds, we were going to uproot ourselves from all that we had grown up with, and cut ties to our lifelong friends and most importantly, our parents and other relatives.

The thought of those times and that decision even today brings tears to my eyes. We missed terribly family times together, our kids growing up with grandparents and cousins, aunts and uncles, etc. We couldn't have family get-togethers any more; we missed high school reunions.

Our parents are now gone and the family broken up and spread across the Country.

My dad was second generation born in Montreal, my mom was born in Halifax but loved living in Quebec until things just became so uncomfortable for them as Anglos that they too had to leave in 1985. They settled in St. Catharines, ON.

My wife's parents also had to leave Montreal about the same time and ended up just east of Toronto, Whitby to be exact.

I have a sister in Halifax, another sister in Niagara Falls (USA) and a brother in Lethbridge. Nancy has a sister in London, ON, a brother in Toronto another brother died recently in Winnipeg and yet another brother in North Vancouver. Although movement in a country such as ours is not unusual I think it is safe to say that if we had not all been driven out of Quebec that is where most of us would still be living-much closer together.

Rod and Nancy Hyslop, Delta, BC

~ • ~

The sentiments of more than a few is expressed in this dandy little letter to the Editor of the National Post (June 18, 2013.)

Congratulations to Ottawa politicians for standing up for Sikhs and demanding that turbans be visible on Quebec Soccer fields. Could a few federal politicians now stand up for Anglo-Canadians in Quebec and similarly demand that English be visible on trucks, buses and billboards?

Keith Henderson, Montreal West, QC

~ • ~

CHAPTER TWENTY

THE ANGLOPHOBE POLITICAL COMPLEX

Kevin Richard tells me, "I'm still clinging to my country but I do understand your sentiment about it being a good time to wave a friendly goodbye to Quebec. I certainly don't blame you or anyone else for coming to this conclusion. I sense that the sentiment is widespread which should be of tremendous concern for Quebecers. It is for me.

A parting of the ways would be extremely difficult for people such as myself (Canadian Quebecers).

I remember the 1995 rally in Montreal quite well. It was extremely touching and it probably saved the country from the damaging ramifications of a "yes" victory. I thank you for the role you played in the union of our nation."

Kevin is responding to some of my questions concerning his editorial entitled **"The Anglophobe Political Complex and Ugly Reminders of Bill 14"** published in the April 2, 2013 edition of the Sherbrooke Record newspaper.

"Exactly what is the Anglophobe Political Complex?" I ask. "Tell me about yourself, your age, your relationship to Quebec, your view of the political situation there."

"I'm 35," replies Kevin, "perfectly bilingual, married, and a father. I was born and raised in the Eastern Townships of Quebec. I was schooled in English; spoke French at home and today work in French. I have strong ties to both the English and French communities in my area. The first time I cast a ballot was in the 1995 referendum."

"Your editorial about the Anglophobe Political Complex is fascinating," I tell him, "but confusing. What is the Anglophobe Political Complex? I've never heard that expression before!"

"The Anglophobe Political Complex," he explains, "is a term I suddenly came up with as a way to identify the group of people I describe in the Sherbrooke Record editorial. They have political clout because they work within political organizations. Their main tactic is fear, by constantly claiming that the French language is in imminent peril. They then present themselves as virtuous for wanting to come to the protection of the French language by using the powerful tool of government force. Their claims, of course, are highly exaggerated. And in my opinion the government should not have the authority to determine issues of language and culture."

Here's what Kevin had to say in his, by now, much-debated editorial in the Sherbrooke Record.

THE ANGLOPHOBE POLITICAL COMPLEX
And the ugly reminders of Bill 14

It only takes a slight change in the direction of the wind in Quebec to go from relative peace and tranquility to political chaos. I enjoyed the quietness while it lasted, but deep down I knew this day was coming.

We're mere months into a PQ government, a minority at that, and the chaos is here. On one hand the government attempts to patronizingly comfort and reassure the Anglophone minority through the minister responsible for the community. But on the other, Anglophones are bitterly reminded that they are not, and never will be, full members of Quebec society.

What happened after so many years of relative peace? Why is there a renewed attack on the English language? The answer is, The Anglophobe Political Complex (APC). Although a minority, the APC is a powerful and influential force in the province. Its goal doesn't stop with sovereignty. It has the added goal of marginalizing Anglophones and perhaps even eliminating all traces of their culture, heritage, and influence in the province.

Make no mistake; this is indeed a large and well-organized minority. Its members are politically active on a vast number of fronts. They control several political parties. They also control activist groups such as la Society St.-Jean Baptise and le Mouvement Quebec francais.

All political parties fear them. The PQ has no other choice but to acquiesce to their demands, otherwise their leader will be quickly disposed of. The Quebec Liberal Party fears them. They tread very carefully so as not to disturb them, otherwise the APC will mobilize and spread their fears to some of the party's supporters.

The CAQ, it seems, is somewhere between the two. They feel the need to appease the APC, as they are, after all, a coalition, and as such they are fragile.

Although the APC may find itself on the back burner from time to time, the simmering always turns to boiling. Consequently, it must be attended to and cooled off. This, of course, necessitates a sacrifice from the English community on the altar of the APC.

This is the spirit that inhabits Bill 14. It is the spirit of all language laws in Quebec. Every year statistics are twisted and used to claim that the French language is in peril. Immediately there is a large-scale APC mobilization effort for a renewed attack on the already dwindling and vulnerable Anglophone minority. The APC claims the language laws are only in self-defense. These laws are dressed up as an honorable, worthy and even virtuous attempt at protecting the French language and culture. The truth however, is that these laws serve nothing more than to quench the thirst of the APC, and in the process it is strengthened and justified. It's only a matter of time before they demand more.

There can be no other reason. Just look around. Here in the Townships, where Anglophones were once prominent, there are only remnants. The slow-kill tactics initiated 40 years ago are working. School (English) enrollment is a fraction of what is once was. The (English) hospital was shut down. Promises were made to have signs in both languages at the CHUS hospital, only to have the language police remove them months later. Some of our towns had their names cleansed from the dirty remnants of the forbidden language. And thus, history is rewritten: "They"...(the English) were never here. In spite of it all, the APC still has the audacity to claim that Anglophones should count themselves lucky for how well treated they are in comparison to Francophones in other provinces.

The fact that this bill (14) is being considered is discouraging. Worse still is that even in the context of a minority government much of it will likely pass. Such is the power of the APC.

Francophones should also be outraged. This bill seeks to limit their access to English CEGEPS. A fully emancipated, Francophone student with outstanding grades will not enjoy the free and equal access to English CEGEPS. This is a violation of equality rights. But once again the virtuous claim of the protection of the French language is made. Even if this was the true motivation (which it is not) the message remains the same: English-speaking people in Quebec are to be viewed as undesirables. Consequently, the PQ government wants to keep real Quebecois from being tainted with the stain of the English language and culture.

According to the APC, once you carry this stain, no matter where you were born, how long you lived here, or the number of generations your family has been here, you can never be a full-fledged Quebecois and this can never be your true home. Full membership and participation is denied. You are merely tolerated and you should count yourself lucky at that. After all, you are an undesirable.

Quebecers should not stand for this. Is it not time to redefine the role of government? Should they even have the power to legislate such things? The only institution with the natural authority to determine the issues of language and culture is the family, not the state. Any attempt by the state to do so violates our right to liberty and our freedom of expression. These are not privileges granted by the state. These are our natural rights! Individual freedom and liberty are much more valuable than the society engineering now taking place.

If we truly value freedom and liberty then this necessarily means that the role of government should be strictly limited to protecting our rights instead of telling us how to speak and how to live.

Quebecers can decide these things for themselves. Once government oversteps these bounds there is no end in sight. We will then be told what to eat, drink, smoke, wear, think, believe and even speak.

It looks like we are already there until there arises a political force that is willing to challenge the power of the Anglophobe Political Complex

Kevin Richard, Ste Catherine-de Hatley, QC

Speculation as I write this is that Bill 14 will not pass in its entirety (at least not this time), but no matter, if this kind of bombshell had been launched 20 years ago, or maybe even ten years ago the reverberations would have been felt from coast to coast.

On April 6, 2013 the National Post said that, *"Quebec's suppression of minority rights is on a scale not matched by any other jurisdiction in any civilized Western democracy."*

Tough words indeed, but in Canada other than a two editorials in the Post, Kevin Richard's comments in the Sherbrooke Record, for the most part, the media and Quebec's "lamb lobby" have hit the mute button.

A couple hundred people showed up at a Montreal protest Bill 14 rally that was disdainfully dismissed by Jean-Francois Lisee, the PQ cabinet minister supposedly in charge of "Anglophone Affairs". Barely able to conceal his distaste for the whole matter Lisee described it as a "rather small rally, comprised mainly of the 'old guard' of Anglophone leadership who carry with them some of the worries from decades past."

"Besides," sniffed the Honourable Member, "in 1995, 80 per cent of Quebec Anglos said they were thinking of leaving the province. Today that is only 42 per cent!"

Put that one in your pipe and smoke it please!

Whether he was aware of the fact that most of the Anglos who wanted to leave in 1995 have already high-tailed it out of the province is not clear. But to the PQ the fact that almost half of the few remaining Anglos want to leave the province is some kind of grand victory!! Boasting material!

But the fact that even that statement was allowed to slip under the radar is further proof that everyone is so worn out by all of this nonsense that if Quebec were to take the final step and actually leave Canada it wouldn't create much of a stir either in the province or out of it. In fact from what I am seeing and hearing these days I suspect instead of sound and fury there would be only a sigh of relief!

I am not alone in suggesting that the Quebec "lamb lobby" has adopted as its theme song "Don't worry, Be Happy"!

On July 24, 2010 the Ottawa Citizen published this article entitled:

CHAPTER TWENTY-ONE

WHERE HAVE ALL THE ANGRY ANGLOS GONE?

By Dave Rogers

English speaking residents of the Outaouais must defend their rights or face marginalization, according to the organization that speaks for them.

In an open letter to the Anglophone community in June, the Regional Association of West Quebecers (RAWQ) asked whether English speakers care that their existence as a community is inadequately recognized by governments and businesses.

"It is important to note that in the Outaouais there are over 58,000 English speaking citizens representing more than 16 per cent of the entire population," said the letter distributed under the heading "Do We Care Anymore."

Recently the question of West Quebecers board of directors has been considering is whether our communities are indeed asleep at the switch or have just thrown in the towel. Indications are that the situation is probably a little bit of both."

Not long ago the attitude of West Quebec Anglophones was far different.

In 1999 a posse of militant Shawville English speakers chased a provincial "language police" inspector out of town during a showdown over French on business signs.

Former Wakefield resident Michael Parasiuk fought a two and a half year legal battle that convinced the Supreme Court of Canada to rule in 2005 that his two children were entitled to English language elementary schooling.

Since then the Conservative government has limited funding available to minority groups for court challenges and Anglophone militants have all but disappeared in the Outaouais.

More young English speakers now learn French well enough to work in both languages and are more interested in blending in than in confrontation.

The association's motto is "A Healthy English Speaking Community is a secure French Speaking Quebec. A strong Quebec is a united Canada."

Richard Turcotte, the new Francophone president of RAWQ, says there have been recent complaints from English-speaking business owners in the Pontiac who were told they must communicate with provincial officials in French.

Shawville spa owner Jennifer Hodgins couldn't understand a notice she received in June from the Quebec equivalent of the Workplace Safety and Insurance Board because she doesn't speak French.

Hodgins said an official from the Commission de la sante et de la securite du travail told her he couldn't explain the notice to her in English because Quebec's language law requires his agency to communicate with its clients only in French.

Meanwhile, RAWQ's membership has slipped to 375 from more than 3,000 during the 1980s.

John Trent, who founded RAWQ in 1981 and served as president, says English speaking Outaouais residents are interested in bargain housing and living the good life. He adds they are usually well served by government and businesses in West Quebec.

"Even the Parti Quebecois, the Block Quebecois and the St. Jean Society have a hard time attracting new members because most young people are bilingual and multicultural and don't understand what the controversy is all about.

"A lot of English speaking people continue living their Ontario lives here in Quebec. For the most part they can get the services in English. When there is not a lot of conflict going on people don't seem to rally to this sort of organization."

Guy Chiasson, a University de Quebec en Outaouais political scientist, said the Quebec language debate has shifted towards immigration and reasonable accommodation of minority groups.

"A lot of English speaking people heave moved to parts of Gatineau, Alymer and Chelsea,"Chiasson said. "These people tend to live their lives in English and some of them work in Ottawa. There is not as much polarization around language as there once was. Recent surveys have shown there isn't much enthusiasm for another referendum."

Former West Quebecers director Brian Gibb said there has been a movement away from English language rights since the 1990s.

"At an institutional level there has been a major shift away from English rights towards community development," Tyler said, "The major thing West Quebecers does is it makes sure that English speaking Quebecers get health and social services delivered to them in English.

"One of the good things that happened is the province opened a community health centre in Hull that helps Anglophones navigate the system.

Gibb is more concerned that Anglophones are doing too little about barriers to English language education in Quebec.

Gibb said the transfer in 2006 of John Paul II High School in Campbell's Bay to a Shawville high school was another sign of the "linguistic cleansing" of Anglophones.

"There is a much larger question that is not being addressed and that is what is the future of English schools," Tyler said. "The underlying question is that Bill 101 is killing the English schools over time.

"The bill prohibits immigrants from sending their kids to English schools, including kids from the United States, Australia and other Commonwealth countries. Less than half of the English speaking kids attend English schools.

English speaking communities across Quebec are in decline or are becoming assimilated partly because in the past several years, eight to ten English schools were closed across the province," Tyler said.

'The community can raise the money itself, but I don't see that happening. There is no real leadership or sense of community across the Outaouais for English speaking people. There have been a number of confrontations in which the English community came out on the losing end and people are tired of going to the barricades".

~ • ~

Can there be any question that the intent of Pauline Marois and her government is to see the Anglo population decline even more? While the rest of Canada embraces, protects and goes out of its way to assist minorities, Quebec is doing everything in its power to further discriminate against minorities, to make life as difficult as possible, not just for those who cannot speak French, but for all non-Francophones. Just ask the parents of children who wish to play soccer while wearing turbans! Do you really think that is an issue of safety? Of course it is not. It is racism of the most blatant and despicable kind. Using kids who just want to play a game as pawns in your war with Canada is disgusting, but sadly only too typical!

And let's never forget, Ms. Marois was very open, very clear about her plans for Anglos during the election campaign. No one could possibly misunderstand her intent to erode minority rights even further. Although I doubt many of us thought her distaste for minorities would prompt her to endorse a ban on turban-wearing soccer kids! Language and headgear seem to really get into her craw don't they?

During the election campaign she went so far as to spell out, step by step how she planned not only to restrict English language rights even further, but also the manner in which she would do all in her power to frustrate and impede the federal government in any way possible.

Quebecers elected her government with full knowledge that she would impose laws and regulations intended to reduce the English-speaking minority even further.

Some might go so far as to say that Quebecers elected a government that openly promised to not only discourage minorities but go so far as to introduce blatant racist policies.

Is there another province in this country whose citizens would knowingly elect a government promising to do everything possible to discriminate against a minority because of the language they speak?

The answer is no. In fact, the citizens of any other province would be outraged at such a suggestion. Once again I invite you to call me if you believe I am wrong.

More than a few residents of Quebec, including family members, have been highly critical of me for writing this book. They point out that they did not vote for the Pauline Marois government but are now stuck with it. "True enough," I tell them, "but you can be sure as hell that many of your neighbours did. Many of your fellow workers too no doubt. Including, by the way, thousands of federal public servants! Figure that one out!"

"Well over a quarter million people have fled the racist policies of Quebec," I remind them. "You have chosen to stay. Those who moved away had to pay a price, a very heavy one in many cases, and you can hardly blame them for being angry. You should not be surprised to learn that some of those forced out of Quebec feel betrayed by those of you who chose to stay.

It may not be fair. It may not make much sense to you. But that's the way it is. That's reality!"

Quebecers knowingly elected a government, headed by Pauline Marois that promised to further discriminate against the tiny English-speaking minority. The voters of no other province would do such a mean-spirited thing.

Sadly, Ms. Marois is one politician who is fulfilling her promises!

CHAPTER TWENTY-TWO

NOW IS THE PERFECT TIME
TO SAY GOODBYE

I present this as further evidence endorsing my argument that now is the perfect time to wave a friendly goodbye to Quebec. Almost all opposition to separation inside and outside Quebec has pretty well petered out. Quebec federalists, still trying to man the walls, are down to a couple rounds of grapeshot. In the rest of Canada, defenders of national unity would be hard pressed to locate a couple rusty muskets to fend off the "Au Revoir Quebec" troops.

As you will read, in a later chapter, even some well-educated young Anglo Quebecers don't believe Canada is a fit partner for the Republic of Quebec. As you will read, there are more than a few English speaking students on our university campus who don't believe the rest of the country will ever be able to catch up to the highly progressive, (in their minds!) much more liberated, vastly superior culture of Quebec, so who are we to hold them back like this?

According to them, and many others, that's very rarified air they breathe in Quebec and until we sharpen up and become much more progressive in the rest of Canada (ROC) we have no right to ask that we be allowed to share any of it!

Hardly anyone in Quebec seems to appreciate the billions of dollars the ROC pours into the province and with taxes now sucking up more than 42 per cent of our pay cheques, if Quebec doesn't really want the money we dump into their laps every year, let's keep the eight or nine billion so we maybe can afford to provide three baths a week for our needy seniors instead of the two they we now dole out!

Well, you say, perhaps Quebec Anglos have given up the fight, but many Francophones are expressing outrage concerning some of Pauline Marois' proposals in Bill 14.

You've got to be kidding! Fact is, there has been precious little concern, let alone outrage, from Francophones concerning the manner in which Bill 101 chased Anglos out of their province. Any Francophone outrage today over Bill 14 has nothing to do with treatment of the English minority. What some Francophone Quebecers are upset over today is the fact that the French ox is being gored!

One of the provisions of Bill 14 would limit Francophone access to English language schools, in particular English CEGEPs. (Junior colleges). French speaking parents know full well that if their children are going to be able to compete in a mostly English speaking global economy they must have access to an English language education. In fact most of the criticism concerning Bill 14 has come from French students and their parents who want to acquire bilingual fluency.

You can be certain that one of the things that will be changed in Bill 14 will be to placate Francophones. Concern for their Anglo neighbours? Not a chance!

CHAPTER TWENTY-THREE

OF BUSINESS CARDS AND SIN

The claim that English is a universal language, spoken everywhere, is not quite accurate.

Debbie and I have a close friend who panicked while touristing along the Great Wall of China. Attracted by some of the items for sale in nearby stalls she wandered away and got lost. Only through the use of sign language was she able to get directions back to the Wall and her husband. "We've travelled the world," she explains, "but for the first time I couldn't find a single soul who could speak English."

I was telling this story to a neighbour the other day when I suddenly realized that as far as I can remember the only time I couldn't find anyone to understand my English was in a funky little Chinese restaurant, in of all places, Vancouver! It's true.

With rare exception, no matter where you go these days you are going to find someone who not only speaks English, but speaks it very well. Which is why, even in the most desperate part of the Middle East or Africa, those protest signs almost always have English as one of the languages.

Which, I am certain, is why our Minister of Foreign Affairs, John Baird has two sets of business cards. One set in English only for presentation when he's in places like London, Geneva, Cairo, Athens, Washington, etc. You get the idea. The second set of business cards for presentation in places like Ottawa, Montreal, Quebec City, Paris, etc. is bilingual. You may understand, but apparently Graham Fraser, our Language Commissioner does not.

The Language Commissioner's report stated that "providing bilingual business cards on some occasions and cards in English only at other times does not foster the promotion of linguistic duality in Canada and abroad and does not express the equality of both official languages which is the heart of Department objectives and stipulated by the Official Languages Act."

His report was dated April 4, 2013 in response to a complaint from NDP official languages critic Yvon Godin.

Baird was given 30 days to fix the "problem". What happens if he does not isn't clear. (30 lashes perhaps? Forced to clean parliamentary toilets with a toothbrush? What?)

Our Foreign Affairs minister isn't the only one to run afoul of our Language Commissioner and the Official Languages Act. International Cooperation Minister Julian Fantino was placed under "investigation" for the crime of instructing that any documents sent to him for review or signing should be in English. Fantino isn't able to read French very well, so in order to save money and time he says just send it to me in English. If it's got to go outside his office translate it into French. Under the Official Languages Act this is apparently some gradation of iniquity. Once again punishment is unclear. (Should we light candles for his misbegotten soul? How many?)

CHAPTER TWENTY-FOUR

DON'T GO WEST!

Then of course there was the Phil Mcneely affair.

Widely know in Ottawa environs as "The alleged" Phil Mcneely, in honour of his uncanny ability to never be seen or heard from for years on end, the Ottawa-Orleans Liberal MPP suddenly burst into full bombast one sunny April morning in 2013, demanding the Language Commissioner stop the Department of National Defense from moving from a location east of the Parliament Buildings to west end Ottawa.

"This," claims McNeely "is a language issue since the bulk of DND employees live in east end Orleans which is 35 per cent Francophone. Forcing them to travel to the west end of Ottawa where the Francophone population is only five or six per cent contravenes the Official Languages Act."

Actually McNeely's letter of complaint to the Language Commissioner says a great deal more than what has been widely reported and more importantly says a great deal about the Official Languages Act and how its tentacles are seeking areas never intended by its original drafters.

The original intent of the Official Languages Act when it was first enacted into law on September 9, 1969 was as it states to: **"ensure respect for English and French and ensure equality of status and equal rights and privileges as to their use in federal institutions."** In other words make sure that taxpayers could communicate with the federal government in either English or French. (It also spells out additional bilingual requirements in a number of other areas, which I'll explain in more detail in the next chapter.)

This decision to formalize an Official Languages Act followed the Bilingualism, Bicultural Commission report launched by the Liberal government of Lester Pearson.

Quite frankly, as I recall, at the time it was not very controversial. Most Canadians, certainly the bulk of those who called my show in those days, believed it was only fair that French speakers should be able to find someone in government to deal with them in the French language just as English speakers were able to find someone to speak English.

There was some concern in some quarters over the provision stating that in certain designated areas, employees of the federal government had a right to work in the language of their choice, but those complainants were usually dismissed as anti-French or simply crackpots.

Prime Minister Pearson and several members of his cabinet appeared on my show more than once to assure Canadians that the Official Languages Act didn't mean everyone in the federal government would have to be bilingual. Mr. Pearson, in fact, very often used the term practical bilingualism. Explaining that if the first person you contacted in his government couldn't speak French or English someone would be found who could. It was also made very clear that in predominantly English-speaking areas of Canada finding someone to speak French might not happen immediately. The same thing could very well happen in mostly French speaking areas of Quebec were finding someone to speak English might involve a reasonable delay.

It all sounded very reasonable. So innocent! As Canadians we puffed our chests out, pridefully considering ourselves very magnanimous and progressive indeed. Far superior again to those damn Yankees!

I recall very distinctly being assured repeatedly that we had to be practical but in the end even if it didn't happen immediately, Canadians had a right to address their federal government in either of the two official languages, French or English.

However, what many Canadians don't know, because it was never widely publicized, is that in 1988 the Mulroney government, in response to provisions in the Charter of Rights and Freedoms, essentially re-wrote the Official Languages Act to greatly broaden its scope. For the first time the Act unsheathed its language tentacles from the confines of government to reach into the daily lives of ordinary people in villages, towns and cities across the country. At least that was the intent. As I will point out later, tentacles that might aid the English speaking population of Quebec have been severed!

With this new and supposedly greatly improved Official Languages Act the Government of Canada entered into an agreement to "**support and assist in the development of official language minority communities**".

According to the Language Commissioner the intention with this new commitment is to enable "English speaking communities in Quebec and French speaking communities in a territory or in a province other than Quebec to thrive and enjoy the same benefits as the rest of the population".

(Some of you will recall those eight deadly words—"I'm here from the government to help you!")

Pretty heady stuff. The result of this amendment is to broaden the powers of the Official Languages Act well beyond the confines of the government itself. Now the government of Canada has a legal obligation to assist minority French and English communities to thrive. It even spells out some of the measures the government must take in order to fulfil its obligations to these minority communities. Obligations that very clearly are not being enforced in Quebec.

It is precisely this segment of the Act (section 41) that Phil McNeely uses to bolster his claim concerning the move of DND to Ottawa's west end.

Furthermore, let me tell you, I'm no lawyer, but when you examine the Act very carefully you have to think that if McNeely really wants to pursue this and gets himself a good lawyer he might just win!! Think of that! Millions spent on purchasing then refurbishing the previous Nortel building only to have a few sentences of the Official Languages Act force the cancellation of the entire move!

I don't for a moment think this will happen, but according to the Act, if a judge determines that indeed the move will cause harm to the Francophone fact in a defined community the possibility does exist! That's how far-reaching the Act has become. How far it has wandered from the original intent of providing equality of language within the federal public service.

McNeely's letter of complaint to the Language Commissioner presents us with a prime example of how the original intent of the Act has been extended and warped to the point where English business cards are outlawed and lawyers investigate whether moving an office from one end of town to another is breaking the law!

As you will see from the McNeely letter below, someone has done his or her homework on this one. As I write this, the Language Commissioner has not yet ruled on the validity of McNeely's complaint, but the mere fact that a legal case can be made that moving DND headquarters to west end Ottawa violates our language laws boggles the mind. At least it does mine!

In fact, as you will see in McNeely's letter, the Official Languages Act, may have played a role in keeping an Ottawa area hospital from closing. A long way indeed from simply making sure we can find someone in government who can speak to us in either French or English!

Let's have a look at how MPP Phil McNeely (Lib) Ottawa Orleans presents his case.

(I have omitted some paragraphs, which are repetitive or deal with arcane legal arguments) The full text is available from the Office of the Language Commissioner).

Dear Commissioner Fraser,

The purpose of this letter is to outline a complaint regarding what I believe to be a violation of s.41 of the Official Languages Act (OLA).

In December 2010, the Department of National Defense (DND) along with Public Works and Government Services Canada (PWGSC) announced the purchase of the Nortel campus on Carling Ave, near Kanata, Ontario. The ultimate aim is to move ten thousand DND employees to the site from their current location mainly in the downtown core in the coming years. It is also expected that a future 10,000 government jobs will be located at a redeveloped Tunney's Pasture in the coming years.

In addition, the Royal Canadian Mounted Police has moved roughly 4,700 employees to a new location in Barrhaven, from their former location just east of Downtown. That move is essentially complete.

I am deeply concerned about the impact that this will have on the Francophone communities in Orleans, the East-End/Vanier and Ottawa as a whole. A large proportion of the affected employees are Francophones or are members of a Francophone household and live in my riding. Given that commuting from the East End or Orleans would be prohibitively costly in time, energy and fuel, many, if not most of those affected, can be expected to move to a community nearer to their place of work. RCMP and DND employees are posted in and out of our city on a frequent basis. They will leave Orleans and their replacements will purchase or rent in Barrhaven or the Kanata areas, as opposed to their traditional choice of Orleans.

It is my belief that the relocation of so many of these employees to the outer edges of the West End, where Francophones represent a much smaller proportion of the population than in the East End, Orleans, or Prescott-Russell, will be seriously detrimental to the vitality of the official language minority communities of those areas and indeed to that of the City of Ottawa as a whole. As such, the measures constitute a violation of the federal governments obligations under s. 41 (1) and 41 (2) of the OLA.

What flows is a more detailed outline of my complaint, which is set out in three parts.

Part I is a summary of the basic facts of the situation, as I understand them

Part II provides an outline of what I understand to be the federal government's obligations in relation to official languages minority communities,

Part III will detail my reasons for thinking that the decision to relocate and consolidate Department of Defense and RCMP staff in the western outer suburbs was made in violation of those obligations.

I. FACTUAL BACKGROUND

(Here McNeely restates the numbers involved in the move to the old Nortel building), then goes on to state:

According to a recent article by Anne Gilbert, Professor of Geography at the University of Ottawa and a specialist in minority Francophone communities in Canada, about 1 in 3 Orleans residents has French as their first language, meaning roughly one third of the total Francophone population of the City of Ottawa (119,445 according to the 2006 census) lives in that community. This makes Orleans particularly important to the vitality and well being of the French language and the Francophone community in the greater Ottawa area.

There is a vast body of social science research demonstrating the importance of territorial concentration to the use and transmission of minority languages. The more a minority is dispersed, the greater the likelihood of language shift towards the majority language. A large part of this effect is due to the absence of lack of access to minority language institutions, such as schools, businesses, churches or other community organizations. Language and identity are acquired through, and transmitted by, the institutional infrastructure of a community, and geographically dispersed minorities often struggle to establish or maintain an adequate degree of "institutional completeness".

This is precisely the reason why the mass urbanization of the 20th Century has been so detrimental to the vitality of the French language outside Quebec. As French speakers left behind unilingual rural communities and moved into urban centers where English was the majority language, they tended to disperse in search of economic opportunity, thereby finding themselves in neighborhoods or communities with few or no existing Francophone institutions and lacking the critical mass of French speakers needed to generate and sustain new ones.

Because of this, neighbhourhoods in which a high concentration of French speakers reside are critical to the survival and flourishing of a city's French language community. The evidence therefore suggests that government policies that tend to disperse French speakers throughout a large urban agglomeration directly undermines the sociolinguistic vitality of the city's Francophone community.

In light of this, the transfer of large numbers of civil service jobs to the predominently English speaking West End and western suburbs can be expected to undermine the vitality of the Francophone community—both in Orleans specifically and across the City as a whole—even though the total number of Francophones in the City of Ottawa or the National Capital Region would remain unchanged.

II. The federal government's obligations towards the Francophone community in Eastern Ottawa-Orleans.

It is my belief that because of the impact described above, the federal government's actions are in violation of the OLA. Most provisions of the OLA have no direct bearing on the matter at hand, since they deal with internal workings of various federal institutions or the services they render to the public. However, Part VII of the Act prohibits the government from engaging in this very type of action.

As you no doubt are aware, after the introduction of the Charter in 1982, Parliament decided to amend the OLA and the overall framework of the federal language policy to reflect the altered Constitutional content and the commitment to substantive equality between French and English. One of the objectives of federal language policy would henceforth be to promote the development of linguistic minorities (i.e., communities of official language speakers whose first language is different from that of the majority in their province). Thus, the preamble to the new version of the Act states that:

The Government of Canada is committed to enhancing the vitality and supporting the development of English and French linguistic minority communities, as an integral part of the two official languages communities of Canada and to fostering full recognition and use of English and French in Canadian society.

Accordingly Section 2 of the OLA now provides that one of the purposes of the Act is to "support the development of English and French linguistic minority communities and generally advance the equality of status and use of the English and French languages within Canadian society". Part V11 of the Act sets out a number of specific provisions dealing with this objective. Of these, s.41 is the most relevant provision for present purposes. It essentially restates the commitment from the pre-amble in the form of a legal obligation.

(Here he includes Section 41 of the Official Languages Act)

(1) The Government of Canada is committed to:

Enhancing the vitality of the English and French linguistic minority communities in Canada and supporting and assisting their development; and

Fostering the full recognition and use of both English and French in Canadian society.

Duty of federal institutions.

Every federal institution has the duty to ensure that positive measures are taken for the implementation of the commitments under subsection (1). For greater certainty, this implementation shall be carried out while respecting the jurisdiction and powers of the province.

Thus, the government is bound by two commitments; to enhance the vitality of official language minority communities and to foster the full recognition of both languages in Canadian society. Furthermore, federal institutions have a duty to take "positive measures" to ensure that the Government of Canada lives up to these commitments.

(Here the McNeely letter enters into some legal arguments stating that the Act must be interpreted broadly and generously, then advances two court cases, one in the Supreme Court of Canada, another by the Federal Court which he says back up his claim that section 41 of the OLA is legally enforceable.)

Then his letter goes on to say: *What is more, the courts have in the past held that the "sociological impact" of a proposed government measure can be used as a basis for striking it down, provided that impact violates a legal duty. In a landmark case the Ontario Court of Appeal upheld a decision of the Superior Court striking down a decision of the Health Services Restructuring commission to limit or eliminate the delivery of health care services through the Montfort Hospital, based on the broader socio-linguistic impact this measure is expected to have.*

The Commission had been set up to restructure the province's entire health care system following major cuts to federal transfer payments that put a great deal of pressure on provincial budgets. As part of its cost cutting measures, the Commission had wanted to close down Montfort Hospital, the only wholly Francophone hospital in Ontario or at least drastically reduce its size. At trial, the court struck down the decision because of the impact of the proposed changes on the rights of the members of the minority Francophone community in Ontario to have their cultural/linguistic heritage respected and protected.

In reaching the conclusion that such an impact made the Commission's decision unlawful, the court started from the premise that with its official language and founding culture status, the minority Francophone culture occupies an enhanced multicultural status. English and French are accorded special status in comparison to other linguistic groups in Canada.

The court therefore concluded that as a matter of Constitutional law, the Commission was required to take into account the hospital's socio-cultural characteristics as an institution, whose existence was of great importance to the continued vitality of Francophone culture in Ontario.

I believe that there is, at this state, a strong prima facie case that the government has breached its obligations under s.41 of the OLA. The proposed changes of location for DND and the RCMP employees would result in a substantial exodus of Francophones from Orleans and other communities east of the city-center with a high density of French speakers, towards a predominantly English speaking part of Ottawa, thereby weakening the demographic and institutional foundations of the Francophone community in those areas and in the National Capital Region as a whole.

Unfortunately, at the present time I lack the resources to carry out a full and thorough study of the impact of these measures will have on Ottawa and Orleans' Francophone community and the vitality of the French language in the affected areas. It is my sincere hope that you will exercise your powers under the OLA to investigate this matter more fully and take appropriate remedial action.

Finally please be advised that because of the seriousness with which I view the threat to the community I represent, I have retained legal counsel—Caza Saikaley srl/LLP—to assist me in the preparation of this complaint and to pursue any and all legal remedies open to me and my community in order to halt these destructive measures

Yours sincerely,

Phil McNeely

So I ask you—who's crazy here? Phil McNeely, or the people who drafted Section 41 of the Official Languages Act, then enacted it into law?

Mind you, I don't think most of us would object so strenuously if this section was applied to the English minority in Quebec. Every effort is made to assist the Francophone communities outside Quebec, but no such effort is made to assist Anglophone communities within Quebec.

You know the situation, it's virtually impossible to obtain a decent job at any level of government and advancement is virtually non-existent unless you are bilingual on the Ontario side of the National Capital and throughout much of eastern Ontario. Forced bilingual signs in places like Russell, etc., but not a peep of protest from the Language Commissioner or anyone else for that matter concerning the "language cleansing" that's been underway in Quebec for decades.

Very clearly the Official Languages Act, just as with official bilingualism and multiculturalism applies only to jurisdictions outside Quebec.

This fact is not lost on a growing number of Canadians who quite frankly are fed up with the hypocrisy and blatant unfairness of the situation. It's one of the reasons why so many Canadians are throwing up their heads in frustration and are now professing a willingness to wave a friendly goodbye to Quebec.

This was made very clear the day the news concerning Phil McNeely's letter broke. My phone lines were jammed with angry callers. Emails poured in.

Here (with minor editing) is a sampling of comments from some of those who provided me permission to use their full names.

CHAPTER TWENTY-FIVE

THE PEOPLE SPEAK

"You can only poke the bear so much and then the backlash will come. English Canada is fed up with Quebec's entitlement society. The sooner Quebec separates the sooner that reality will sink in when they realize there will be no transfer payment, no more cheap daycare and tuition fees.

Allen R. Thompson, Ottawa, ON

~ • ~

Bilingualism is the biggest fraud that has been ever forced on Canadians. First of all, even if you are English and speak perfect French you are not classed as bilingual. The French test for English speakers is in Parisian French, not Quebec French and they just upped the standard. In my working days in Ottawa it did eliminate me from a job when I had all the requirements except bilingualism. A Quebecer won out even though he was lacking in other requirements.

Pete McLellan, Brockville, ON

~ • ~

I work at the hospital here in Ottawa where nearly every other car in the employee parking lot has Quebec plates. All of the cleaning and repair staff is French speaking—most can barely speak English. Ontario, whether bilingual or not, is on its way to self destruction by creating an environment depriving its own tax paying residents of lucrative full time jobs and giving them instead to Quebec residents who don't live or shop here, leaving our own residents struggling to find work and sucking the social system dry. Totally ridiculous. I cannot believe we are accepting discrimination of our own people!

Natasha Vaz, Ottawa, ON

~ • ~

What about English speakers living in Ontario but forced to work for the government in Gatineau. I believe that linking the French language to the moving of any office building is going too far. There has never been an outcry from the public against the oppression going on against the English in Quebec. This nonsense has to stop!

Kay Matthews, Ottawa, ON

~ • ~

With regards to the move of federal employees to the city's west end, I think we need to find the real underlying problem. MPP McNeely is more concerned about the effects on the Orleans economy and businesses if thousands of his residents move out to the west end. He is trying to use the language issue as leverage in an attempt to put a stop to it. Follow the money! (and the voters). In this case it's all heading west.

Todd O'Rourke, Ottawa, ON

~ • ~

It is outrageous that English speaking government workers must put up with the lack of English services in the community when working in government offices in Gatineau. Some of us have to commute great distances to get to work but would never consider moving to Quebec where we would be oppressed by Francophones. It's another reason to let Quebec leave Canada. We could also save billions by doing away with bilingualism.

Michael Pongray, Barrhaven, ON

~ • ~

Bilingualism in Ontario is completely biased. My fiancée is a college educated water/waste water technician. She doesn't speak French so even in Ottawa with its terrible reputation of dumping raw sewage into the Ottawa River she can't get a job. So we're leaving Ottawa. See ya. We'll be fine. Build a life and pay property tax someplace more tolerant. Thanks.

James St. Louis, Ottawa, ON

~ • ~

I cannot begin to convey how frustrated I am about the Orleans Francophone complaint from McNeely. As a 23-year-old recent graduate with two university degrees, including a bachelor of education, most of my work experience is as a part time student in the federal public service. Unfortunately because my French is limited I cannot find full time employment in the public service. So to hear people who have won the pension lottery, which by the way my generation will never see, complain about a half hour drive makes me shake my head in disbelief. And some people think it's my generation that has a sense of entitlement!!

Lowell, what about Elections Canada moving their headquarters to Hull from downtown Ottawa? Why don't I get Pierre Polievre on the phone demanding some English rights? Hell, I worked with people with zero university education hired because their main skill was the ability to speak French. Shameful. Let them separate so we can get some jobs back.

Michael McAnulty, Ottawa, ON

~ • ~

The truth is, Canada is not a bilingual country. Quebec does not provide any government services in English. Really, what more needs to be said. The rest of Canada has believed their politicians for years, when they claimed that providing French-speaking people complete access to French services in the workplace was a good idea. History has proven it may have worked for Quebecers, but no one else. Please people wake up!

Michael David White, Ottawa, ON

~ • ~

Mr. McNeely it is no secret you mostly hide in the weeds and now have chosen to pop up in this most odious fashion by opposing DND's move to the Nortel campus. This is retail politics at its worst, designed to play to your Francophone base. Do you care a whit about the number of Anglophones who have to haul out of their communities all over the City to work in Gatineau? This is about choice and fairness. Those who choose to move west will move west; those who don't will remain in Orleans. It is as simple as that and you know it. Your complaint to the Official Languages Commissioner will have no traction (nor should it) except to fan the flames of division. In other words, this dog won't hunt!

Heather D. Ottawa, ON

~ • ~

Having spent nearly three decades in the RCAF from 1963 to 1990 and another 16 years with Corrections Canada, it was obvious that French speakers have taken over both organizations. I left the RCAF in 1990 as a warrant officer because it was highly unlikely that I could advance in rank because of my lack of French. I am still working at the age of 69 and have occasional contact with CFB Trenton and CFB Kingston.

When dealing with the military in both locations it's sometimes difficult to find anyone who can speak English. It's the same in Corrections Canada. Anyone who has passed the French language test gets paid more than us poor souls that have only English. Not a big amount more, but that extra $800 a year they get is pure discrimination. Also I am sure you are aware of the French language school in Ottawa. I won't mention names but its well known some senior CSC "fat cats" on the verge of retirement get to attend this French language school for about one year simply to extend their stay with CSC so they can rake in their inflated pay cheques. Upon graduation they hang around just long enough to accept their golden handshakes, but never have the opportunity of using the French language we just paid so much for them to be trained in.

Don Smith, Kingston, ON

~ • ~

It is time for Quebec to go its own way. I can't wait for them to leave. Switzerland has five official languages. Each one is accepted and respected by the government and the people and each citizen is free to use it in any way and everywhere he or she pleases. No "generosity" or legislation is involved. Just common sense. There are no minorities, only citizens of equal rights!

Manfred Feese, Ottawa, ON

~ • ~

My name is Denzil Ferguson a 20-year town councilor for Pakenham/Mississippi Mills. I was front and centre when we challenged Canada Post regarding language issues in our small local post office and I am more than prepared to support any initiative in support of a language challenge.

Thank you

Denzil Ferguson, Pakenham, ON

P.S. I am boiling sap or would take the time to call!

~ • ~

(He refers to December 2009 when Canada Post tried four times to kick Packenham Postmistress Jeanne Barr out of her job because she was not bilingual. All post offices within the National Capital region are legislated to have bilingual service even though the latest census indicates there are only 25 people in all of Mississippi Mills who claim to speak only French.

Each time Jeanne was told she was out of a job the community and in particular the town council and the media, including myself, raised bloody hell. More than 750 people signed a conventional petition. An additional 550 people signed an on line petition which is pretty well the adult population of Pakenham.

After telling her on four separate occasions that she was going to be replaced by a bilingual person Canada Post, bowing to local pressure finally agreed to let Jeanne keep her job. One of the things that may have prompted some common sense from Canada Post was a threat from Denzil Ferguson and other councilors to move the post office a short distance away out of the region governed by the NCC!)

~ • ~

English people need to stand up for themselves. We are put on the back burner constantly, McNeely needs to go back to sleep.

Pat Gordon, Ottawa, ON

~ • ~

I moved here from Montréal in 1966. Best thing I ever did. I wish Quebec would separate and Canada should stop being officially bilingual. By the way I speak functional French since my business was in the east end of Montréal and all my clients were French speaking.

Jack Klain, Ottawa, ON

~ • ~

I am writing to provide some input you may choose to use in your book. My wife and I are now looking to move from Quebec even though we both fully bilingual. I was raised in Alymer QC and we bought our home here together more than 20 years ago, during which time we have seen a great deal of change. While we love this place, the political situation rubs me the wrong way.

Every year we attend Winterlude in Ottawa and get a bus in Gatineau to head to the Rideau Canal and back. The evacuation notice on the bus window caught my eye. The English version is half the size of the French so I ask what does safety have to do with language laws? It gives you that sick feeling of being unwelcome and I wonder how the visiting public must feel? This, along with all the other mostly petty laws and regulations.

We have no doctors here in the province. The roads and bridges are falling apart but we spend money on language police and of course the sad story of corruption now pouring out of the Montreal Charbonneau Inquiry!

How does making one province purely French going to work? Why keep the population ignorant of the fact that two or more languages will get you a lot further in life? A truly bilingual education will profit not only Quebec but also all of Canada.

Denis Villeneuve, Alymer, QC

~ • ~

I am one of the many thousands forced out of my home and my business in Montreal when the tongue troopers made life so miserable for my company and our employees that I just closed up shop-lost almost everything and moved to Kingston. Thank goodness my wife and I have been able to re-start our lives and our business, but I will never forgive the racist policies, which as I am sure you know, forced not only my family— but many of our friends and relatives out of the province.

The worst part of it was that even as the trickle of escapees from the province became a flood, no one, and either in Quebec or elsewhere seemed to give a damn. My company was a small one, employing at most two dozen people—but those jobs and tens of thousands of others left Quebec never to return and now of course the province pleads poverty and demands that the rest of the country help it out.

I am sorry to say this, I know it sounds bitter, but to be frank with you and your readers, if Quebec were ever to leave Canada not many tears would be shed in my family.

James Rutherford, Kingston, ON

~ • ~

How many times have we sung our national anthem? We keep pledging to stand on guard for Canada. Well, my Canada includes Quebec. We should never consider the separation of that wonderful province. Separatists should not be encouraged. You may quote me anywhere, anytime.

Bob Paterson, Ottawa, ON

~ • ~

I've thought about this long and hard and have finally come to the conclusion that separation will occur sooner or later. It is only natural that people wish to assemble with those of the same language and culture.

It is true that people of divergent languages and cultures can co-exist with some comfort in countries such as Switzerland and to a degree in Belgium, but if you examine history, including recent history you see that whenever people of a specific language and culture are assembled in one particular region that region inevitably separates from the whole to form its own nationhood.

We have countless examples from the British colonies, almost all of which broke away to form their own countries to more recently the Czech Republic and Slovakia which went their separate ways peacefully and sadly Yugoslavia where the various cultures, languages and religions hived off in violent fashion to form their own countries.

It is after all, only natural to want to live, work and play with and be governed by people who speak your language, understand your culture and share similar values.

Hector Blackwell, Toronto, ON

~ • ~

Separation. Never! Yes, My Country Includes Quebec and I pray to God it always will. I was born and raised in Quebec, speak perfect French and am disgusted that my fellow Canadians for the most part are just too damn lazy and resentful to learn the language. Shame on you all for even suggesting that Canadians don't want Quebec. And as for any money that we pay Quebec, it is well spent. That province represents the very best of this country. Without Quebec we are nothing but a sorry northern version of the United States. Who wants that?

Heather Browning, Ottawa, ON

~ • ~

I send this with great trepidation—but here it goes.

As a member of the Canadian Forces, I have been and will be told again that I have to uproot and move as required by the needs of the

Service. I fully accept this, as this is what I have signed up for. I could receive a message today saying that I'm posted to Quebec and unless I decide to retire early, I will have to accept it. I'm Anglophone with a very basic understanding of French, but I will adapt and deal with the outright bigotry and discrimination that my wife and I will inevitably face should I have to move to Quebec. Those who have gone whining to Mr. McNeely about how hard done by they will be due to what is basically a mere 20 minute increase to their daily commute should realize just how good they have it on this side of the River compared to the other side!

Major Ian Logan

~ • ~

I think most Anglo-Canadians are getting quite fatigued with the whole bilingualism issue and especially when politicians like Mr. McNeely, use the race card to further the Francophone agenda. Quebec has made it perfectly clear it does not want any other culture and language other than French to the point of sheer racism. Canada is not a bilingual country, nor should it be. Mr. McNeely's claim that the move of DND to the west end of Ottawa would cause undue hardship on the Francophones from Orleans is astonishing. There is no requirement for these individuals to move to the west end and out of their present neighbourhood. Just a bit longer commute to their jobs. At least they have jobs!

Anne Blimkie, Rideau Ferry, ON

~ • ~

As spokesperson for Canadians for Language Fairness, I can assure you that by far the majority of complaints that McNeely represents are coming from the former Quebecois who have moved into Ontario.

There are truly some victims of forced bilingualism. Many. But they are English speaking, not French. However, Official Languages czar Graham Fraser absolutely refuses to meet with those true victims. He will only represent the minority point of view if that view is from those who speak French.

The rumblings have been continuously increasing in volume in eastern Ontario, especially since 2008. Our youth east of Ottawa, even though graduates of full French immersion programs are heading west because they just aren't "French" enough. Ontario is losing its young people because they are becoming disenchanted and resentful of having good jobs denied to them simply because someone determines that their French just isn't good enough.

Lowell this is not just about bilingualism. It's about burying our British ancestry, which will also bury our rights and freedoms that have come to us thanks to our heritage. Why do our language laws protect only one language and not both of them? Quebec is applauded and supported in its determination to preserve its language and culture while those of us trying to preserve our language and culture on this side of the River are called racists and worse!

Beth Trudeau, Embrun, ON

~ • ~

I would support the idea of an independent and separate Quebec as long as those who wish to remain loyal Canadian citizens be allowed to do so. You have talked in the past about dual citizenship in the event of Quebec separation. An excellent idea with one proviso. You should not be able to live in Quebec and work in any capacity for the Federal Government of Canada. Otherwise, I say okay. In fact, we would probably all be a lot happier as two separate nations and get along a lot better than we do today. Separation is probably inevitable anyway so let's get it out of the way and get on with our lives.

Jonathan Swinton, Mission, BC

~ • ~

CHAPTER TWENTY-SIX

IS IT JUST ENGLISH BIGOTRY?

I received several hundred more emails but the ones I have included here are a very representative sampling of the sentiment shared, I am certain, not only by the great majority of my listeners, but most English speaking Canadians who have rubbed up against or bumped into our warped and highly discriminatory language laws.

There are some, and I have heard this many times on my show, who would have you believe that those who complain about Quebec and bilingualism are narrow minded, bigoted or worse, and no doubt some are, but bigotry is not confined to one culture or language group.

But when weighing the arguments and the motives of these respondents, please keep this in mind, More than 280,000 Anglos have fled Quebec while today 42 per cent of those who remain in the province say they are thinking of leaving.

No such exodus exists in the opposite direction!

It's not unlike the situation in Cuba. Every time someone extols the virtues of socialism or even in some cases communism I point out that while thousands of people have died trying to escape from Cuba, to my knowledge there has not been a single instance of anyone even getting slightly damp trying to get in!

Do you suppose there is a possibility that when tens of thousands of people uproot themselves, sell homes at distress prices, leave friends, jobs and sometimes family to escape a country or province, there might be some solid reasons?

Surely you wouldn't suggest that all those Anglos left Quebec only because they were bigoted? Out of more than 300,000 Anglos and Allophones who fled Quebec it only stands to reason that at least a few of them were honest, hard working, decent, and non-bigoted! Many of them spoke perfect French and used it in their every day lives. Why do you suppose they fled Quebec? Could it be that laws and attitudes made life so miserable or downright impossible that they had no choice but to leave? What do you suppose would be the reason for that?

Those who fled often refer to themselves as Quebec refugees and when you talk to as many of them as I have over the years you cannot help but conclude that, as far as many of them are concerned, Quebec today has become a racist society where as Kevin Richard wrote in the Sherbrooke Record, "English speaking people are viewed as undesirables!"

Then of course is the fact that at least some of the Francophones agitating for their language rights in Ontario have come from Quebec where they voted for and supported governments that essentially drove the Anglos out. By no means does this apply to all Francophones in Ontario. Of course not, but there is some truth to the argument that more than a few Quebecers voted for separatist candidates and supported discriminatory language laws, and then when tens of thousands, including many business people fled the province, taking jobs with them, some of those Quebecers followed the Anglos into Ontario and are now trying to obtain the same kinds of rights and privileges for themselves that they denied Anglos where they were in Quebec! Beautiful isn't it?

Beth Trudeau in her email claims that most of the agitation for more language rights in eastern Ontario comes from former Quebecers. While she doesn't say it in as many words the implication is clear. There's a very good chance that some of those former Quebecers are now demanding the same kind of minority language rights for Francophones in Ontario that they helped to deny Anglophones in Quebec!

I had a phone call several months ago from a woman who runs a small business in a small eastern Ontario town caught up in the Russell Township language war. " Lowell," she told me, "you may not believe this, but one of the people who is harassing me because I don't have a French sign in front of my store is a well known Quebec separatist who moved here only about a year ago. This guy is a federal public servant who campaigned for the Bloc Quebecois candidate in the last election; now he's over here screaming about discrimination. Can you imagine? Not only that, but he's managed to convince a few Anglos around here that he's the great champion of equal rights and I'm the asshole!"

CHAPTER TWENTY-SEVEN

THE GREAT RUSSELL LANGUAGE WAR!

As further evidence of the manner in which the Official Languages Law is being used to protect and enhance the French language while turning a blind eye to discrimination against those who speak English let's examine what happened in a lovely little chunk of rural Ontario just to the south and east of Ottawa.

They don't call it the Russell language war for nothing.

Because that's pretty well what it was and to some extent still is—a bitter war fought, just as in Quebec, over language. A war that sadly has pitted neighbour against neighbour, friend against friend, even in some cases father against son.

For generations, French, English and Dutch farmed the fertile flatlands of the lower Ottawa Valley at peace with each other in growing prosperity. Even today Russell Township lays claim to being the leading dairy producer of eastern Ontario.

Over the years the towns and villages in the area—Embrun, Russell, Brisson, Marionville and Forget became largely bedroom communities as an ever-increasing number of federal public servants looking to escape the hustle and bustle of the big city (Ottawa) headed for bucolic small town life.

Ten or 15 years ago, the English speaking population comprised only five to ten per cent of the total, but the census of 2006 provides a graphic illustration of what is happening throughout all of eastern Ontario. As more and more Anglos move into the area, the percentage of Francophones continues to drop until today in Russell Township with a population of about 15,000, the split is almost 50-50. In eastern Ontario as a whole those who list French as their mother tongue has dropped from almost 24 per cent in 1971 to only about 16 per cent today.

Whatever the percentages, eastern Ontario and in particular Russell Township have always been models of bilingualism, mutual respect and co-operation. Many who live there have some degree of ability in both French and English; almost everyone in business is fluently bilingual. As any businessperson in the area will tell you, it only makes sense to be able to talk to your customers in their language. And if, by chance you run across someone having difficulty with the language, you can be sure they'd work it out somehow. No big deal!

That's the way it used to be and in some cases still is. These are, after all, for the most part, down to earth common sense people. Well most of them!

But despite the good will and the compromise you will still find in Russell Township things aren't quite the same.

Because right smack dab in the middle of this little island of sanity, peace and plenty someone dropped the "bomb". The "language bomb", fashioned, polished and perfected in Quebec!

Karen Selick, the litigation director for the Canadian Constitution Foundation summed the situation up very well in the following article she wrote for the National Post in June of 2012.

The language police come to Ontario
By Karen Selick

The wish of some Ontario Francophones to live in a fantasy world regarding the importance of the French language outweighs their neighbour's Charter right to freedom of expression—according to the Ontario Court of Appeal.

Okay, okay—that's not quite how the court put it. But that is nevertheless the essence of last week's decision in the case of Jean-Serge Brisson and Howard Galganov against Russell Township.

Four years ago 70% of the commercial signs outside businesses in Russell Township were bilingual. For a group of Francophone zealots 70% wasn't enough. They entreated town council to make bilingual signs mandatory for all businesses.

'The proposal was highly controversial for both Anglophones and Francophones. Two local chambers of commerce opposed it. A committee struck by Council recommended against it. Nevertheless, Council passed the by-law in a three to two vote. It required all new exterior commercial signs to be bilingual with the dimensions and style of lettering being identical in both French and English.

Jean-Serge Brisson owns a radiator repair shop in Russell. Despite being fully bilingual, Brisson erected a non-compliant sign with his business name solely in English and his services listed solely in French. Brisson then challenged the by-law, together with bilingual Anglophone Howard Galganov who had posted a sign written entirely in French.

The two were slapped down by Justice Metivier of the Superior Court of Justice in a 2010 judgment that I described in an article back then as "disturbingly illogical". Unfortunately last week's decision from the Ontario Court of Appeal was not much better.

The Court of Appeal did at least correct one error made by the lower court. It correctly held that the bylaw violated citizens' rights to freedom of expression under the Canadian Charter of Rights and Freedoms. Freedom of expression includes the right not to express oneself in a particular language. "Freedom consists in an absence of compulsion," they wrote, quoting the Supreme Court of Canada.

But then, astonishingly, they said they said that the violation was justified under Section 1 of the Charter—the section that allows governments to violate fundamental freedoms if the violations are within "reasonable limits—demonstrably justified in a free and democratic society."

The appellate court seemed completely hoodwinked by evidence that confused the behaviour of free citizens acting voluntarily with the behaviour of dragooned citizens acting under state coercion. For instance, the court accepted the expert opinion of a bureaucrat with the eastern Ontario French School Board to the effect that "the by-law indicates that the French language has value in the community outside of schools and family life."

Nonsense. When the Francophones of Russell henceforth see business signs in both official languages, they will no longer know whether anyone inside can actually talk to them in French. They will no longer know whether the "bienvenue" genuinely welcomes them, or is merely an artifact of coercion forced upon the unwilling—and possibly resentful— Anglophone or Allophone. Anyone who accepts this an indication that French is either valued by the sign's proprietor or valuable in communicating with him is accepting an illusion—a fraud—manufactured by Russell's town council.

The inference that French is valued by businesses could not validly be drawn unless business chose voluntarily to use that language.

Another expert gave his opinion that the bylaw is a "symbolic recognition of the equality of the French and English languages and cultures." Symbolic indeed! Symbolic and false!

The truth is—and the court had these facts before them—that the use of the French language at home in eastern Ontario decreased from 23.8% of the population in 1971 to a mere 15.6% in 2006. If the Francophone population themselves lack the motivation or wherewithal to keep their numbers up, why should other people be coerced into maintaining the illusion of parity for them? Is phony symbolism really an important enough objective to override a freedom that is so important to Canadians that it is enshrined in our Constitution?

Also, absent from the decision was any explanation of how the by-law, which would force Brisson to add English to his mostly French sign, achieves the goal of promoting or preserving the French language. Charter jurisprudence requires that Section 1 overrides be rationally connected to their objective, but this connection can only be described as irrational.

The decision contains other leaps of illogic too numerous to discuss here. One can only hope that Brisson and Galganov will be able to mount an appeal to the Supreme Court of Canada and that the SCC will place greater value on a Constitutional freedom than on a charade designed to mollify some busybodies' wounded pride.

~ • ~

CHAPTER TWENTY-EIGHT

WHO WON?

What Karen Selick failed to mention is that court costs for the taxpayers of Russell Township are estimated to be well in excess of $100,000. In fact some reports indicate the figure is probably closer to $200,000. No small burden for a tax base of only a few thousand!

And to what purpose? A few more bilingual signs but a whole lot more dissension? How has life been improved for anyone in Russell Township? Has mutual respect been enhanced? Do French and English speaking citizens get along any better? Do they like each other more? Has commerce been improved? Is anyone being served any better in local stores? Have the French language and culture been enhanced? How?

And by the way, have you ever heard any of these French-speaking Russell Township language zealots come to the defense of English language rights in Quebec? You must be kidding!

This is the kind of silly but destructive nonsense that is driving many Canadians, including more than a few Francophones, absolutely crazy. It is why more and more Canadians outside Quebec are beginning to realize that the there will never be peace until Quebec finally bucks up its courage and takes the final step and cuts the cord.

Or, as I am suggesting may have to happen, the ROC is presented with an opportunity to perform the snip job, and provides a gentle but firm push out the door!

Would we see less of this kind of idiocy with an independent Quebec? Probably not entirely, the world is full of foolishness, but I tell you this, every day we're seeing more and more Canadians who wouldn't mind finding out!

CHAPTER TWENTY-NINE

THE OFFICIAL LANGUAGES ACT

Robert Burns didn't have Canada's Official Languages Act in mind when he wrote that famous line about mice and the best laid plans of men, but he could have. Because there is little doubt the Act was drafted with the best of intentions back in 1969. Assuring Canadians access to the federal government in French or English was—well it was the Canadian thing to do.

With some justification, French Canadians felt they were not being treated fairly prior to passage of the Act. Even though at the time they comprised almost 25% of Canada's population, Francophones only occupied nine per cent of jobs in the federal public service. Stories of them being treated rudely when they tried to find someone in government to speak in French were commonplace. They had no legal right to have federal court cases conducted in French, although it was common practice.

So, with the very best of intentions, and with the support of the majority of Canadians, we passed the Official Languages Act and sat back to watch equality and justice, peace and plenty, perhaps even manna from heaven break out. Most of all we couldn't wait for

Quebecers to wrap their arms around Canada, give it a big hug and propose a renewing of our marriage vows.

Unfortunately it didn't turn out quite that way, at least not for all.

For sure, Francophones got far more public service jobs and everything else promised in the Act, but instead of a big thank you, hugs and kisses and maybe even a bottle or two of single malt scotch, the country was treated to things like the FLQ, Bill 101, the War Measures Act, troops in the streets, referendums, the Meech and Charlottetown fiascos, greatly heightened separatist agitation, a mass exodus of Anglos out of the province and lectures from the Language Commissioner about how badly we are treating Francophones!

If I have missed anything call me!

By no means can you blame the Official Languages Act for all the problems inherent in keeping our two languages and cultures from going for each other's throats since the Plains of Abraham. If you examine what's happening around the world you have to marvel at the fact that we've kept it all together with some degree of cordiality this long.

In fact, if enforced as intended, equally across the Country, the Act could very well have saved us a lot of grief, perhaps even have prevented that mass exodus of Anglos from Quebec.

What has happened, sadly, is that the provisions of the Act passed in 1969 and amended in 1988, guaranteeing equal status for both official languages, are today being applied only in provinces outside Quebec. Despite what the Act and The Charter of Rights and Freedoms mandate, in Quebec none of their provisions apply to the status of the English language or non-French speaking Quebecers.

Let's go the website of the Office of the Commissioner of Official Languages and read directly from a section entitled "Your Language Rights".

Our Language Commissioner states that, the purpose of the Act is to:

ensure respect for English and French and ensure equality of status and equal rights and privileges as to their use in federal institutions.

support the development of English and French linguistic communities.

Advance the equal status and use of English and French.

Let me ask you.

(1) Do you see any evidence that there is any attempt on behalf of the Language Commissioner or anyone else to ensure respect for English in the province of Quebec?

(2) Do you see any evidence of attempts by the Language Commissioner or anyone else to support the development of English linguistic communities in Quebec?

(3) Do you see any evidence of attempts by the Language Commissioner, or anyone else, to advance the equal status and use of English in Quebec?

Feel free to call me anytime with your answers!

The Official Languages Act as originally passed in 1969 applied only to federal institutions, including Crown corporations. In addition, some organizations such as Air Canada and VIA rail retained their federal language obligations after they were privatized, but as we have already pointed out there was a subtle change to this when the Act was redrafted in 1988 to obligate the federal government to **"support the development of English and French linguistic communities and advance the equal status and use of English and French."**

This section of the Act is now being used to by some (e.g., Phil McNeely) in an attempt to compel the federal government to support, financially and otherwise, French linguistic communities outside Quebec, but I can see no evidence that any attempt is being made to provide the same kind of support to English speaking communities within Quebec.

This inequity extends beyond the purview of the federal government. As we have seen from decisions handed down in the Russell Township language wars, Ontario courts are prepared to override the Charter of Rights and Freedoms in order to present a "symbolic recognition of the equality of French and English language and culture".

In Quebec, on the other hand, the provincial government overrode the Charter of Rights and Freedoms in order to destroy the equality of the English language and culture and no court has ever attempt to restore that equality, despite what the Official Languages Act mandates!

There's another part of the Act that many Canadians don't believe is being administered fairly.

Section VI mandates that English-speaking and French-speaking Canadians not be discriminated against based on ethnic origin or first language learned when it comes to employment or advancement in the federal public service.

Ask almost any Anglophone who has worked for the federal government since the Act was enforced and they will bend your ear for hours with horror stories about the manner in which those born into English speaking families are discriminated against in the workplace. If you don't speak and write French with great fluency you're pretty well up the creek—any creek— without the proverbial paddle—is their almost universal complaint.

Some of the complaints may very well be just sour grapes. There is no question that some government jobs do require a very high level of French ability, and not every English-speaking employee is the sharpest knife in the drawer, but the complaints from Anglos are so universal you simply cannot dismiss them all.

It is clear to anyone who dares to listen that here is another area of the Official Languages Act that favours those born into French-speaking households and openly discriminates against those from the great majority of Canadian homes where English is the only language spoken.

The discrimination is especially blatant against unilingual Caucasian men. The jokes about unilingual English guys having a better chance of winning the lottery than getting a job with the federal government are no joke at all!

Among other things, of course this pretty well disqualifies most people born west of the Ottawa River unless you are fortunate enough to having been raised in one of the French speaking enclaves of northern Ontario or parts or Manitoba. The fact is, most people born west of the Ottawa River don't even bother applying for a job in Ottawa. They've probably never had the opportunity to even hear French being spoken, let alone had the chance to learn it themselves.

Again, so much for the Official Languages Act assuring equality for all!

And once again I have to ask the question would any of this change if the ROC (rest of Canada) voted Quebec out of Confederation? The answer is that with Quebec no longer part of Canada, thousands of highly paid federal government jobs would almost immediately open up for ROC Canadians, unilingual English or not.

CHAPTER THIRTY

HYPROCISY IN THE WORKPLACE!

I have pointed out that the stated intent of the Official Languages Act is not to force bilingualism on every Canadian, nor compel every federal employee to be bilingual. But if you read the act, and in particular the sections dealing with the language of work it begins to slowly down on your that if all requirements of the Act are adhered to, sooner or later just about everyone who works for any level of government in the National Capital region, eastern Ontario, New Brunswick, northern Ontario, and Manitoba is going to have to be fluently bilingual. It is certainly true of anyone in management.

The following statements are taken directly from the official website of Language Commissioner Graham Fraser.

You tell me if you see the same contradictions, the same hypocrisy that I do.

Part 1V, sections 21 to 33)

The Official Languages Act does not require every Canadian to speak both official languages. On the contrary, the Act aims to ensure that the

Government of Canada is able to provide services to English and French-speaking Canadians in the language of their choice. Approximately one third of federal institution offices must provide services in both official languages. These services must be available without delay and must be of equal quality, regardless of the language chosen by the citizen.

You have the right to communicate with the head or central office of a federal institution in the official language of your choice.

Some of the other offices and facilities of federal institutions are also required to provide services in both languages if:

They are located in the National Capital Region or in a region where there is significant demand for a given language: or

It is reasonable to do so due to the nature of the office

Active offer

To ensure that members of the public know they have the right to use the official language of their choice when dealing with federal institutions, the institutions are required to actively offer services in both languages. The requirement consists of informing the public that services are available in both official languages. This includes answering the telephone in both languages and posting bilingual signs.

How do we determine whether an office is required to provide services in both official languages?

To assess whether demand for service in the language of the minority is significant, we take into account the size of the population belonging to the linguistic minority in the region.

Moreover, an office may be required to provide services in both official languages if its mandate is related to the health and safety of the public, or if it is deemed reasonable for it to do so due to its location or its national or international mandate.

Language of work

Part V, sections 34 to 38)

Regardless of whether they occupy a bilingual position, employees of federal institutions have the right to work in the official language of their choice in the following designated bilingual regions:

New Brunswick

The greater Montreal region

Parts of the Eastern Townships, Gaspe and western Quebec

The National Capital Region

Part of eastern and northern Ontario

Having the right to work in your own language means, for instance:

having work tools (such as reference books, manuals, keyboards, computer software and telephone systems) in your own language

having access to training in your own language

being able to speak in your own language during meetings

feeling free to use your language of choice with your supervisor and with senior management.

In addition to ensuring that these rights are respected, federal institutions are also required to ensure that the work environment is truly conducive to the use of both official languages.

Some signs of a truly bilingual workplace:

Employees participate fully in their professional life and work together in the official language of their choice

Senior management and supervisors lead the way by frequently using both official languages

The organization's workplace culture fully reflects the equal status of both official languages

Employees are proud to work in an environment where using both official languages is valued and encouraged

Managers and staff know their language rights and obligations

Seems very clear to me that despite the claim that only one third of federal institution offices must provide services in both official languages, the overwhelming majority of those in the federal public service must be fluently bilingual, certainly if you want any kind of promotion or are in any sort of managerial role.

Think of it. The Act very clearly states that if you work for the federal government in New Brunswick, Montreal, parts of the Eastern Townships, Gaspe, western Quebec, the National Capital region or parts of eastern and northern Ontario you have the right to work in French or English. Furthermore, your managers and supervisors must be able to communicate with you in either language. More than that, the managers must promote the use of both languages and you have the right to speak either language in all meetings.

Exactly what are the ramifications of this?

Well, first let's have a look at some figures here.

To begin with, about 43 per cent of all federal public servants work in the National Capital Region. About another 25 per cent work in other areas designated areas where public servants have the right to work in the official language of their choice. In addition, close to 75 per cent of all those in managerial and supervisory positions work in the National Capital Region.

Do the math.

Despite what the Act says about not all federal public servants having to be bilingual, the some 70 per cent of those who work in bilingual designated areas will be in workplaces where both languages are being spoken, and all managers and supervisors in those areas will have to be fluently bilingual.

Since some of those in the workplace in those areas will be speaking French, common sense dictates that in order to run an efficient office with everyone working together, everyone is going to have to speak French. And since some of those in the office will be speaking English, it means if there is to be any efficiency everyone is going to have to be able to speak English. There can be no question concerning all those in supervisory and managerial positions. In other words, while the workplace may not be designated bilingual the Act virtually compels it to be.

Since it is a fact that those growing up in Quebec have a much better chance of learning both languages very well then say those from, St. John's, Halifax, Toronto, Brantford, Winnipeg, Regina, Calgary, Vancouver, etc. It doesn't take a genius to see what prompts complaints that Anglos don't stand a chance of promotion or even of being hired.

Advantage Quebec! Big advantage!

While it's not a matter of significant importance in the West, my guess is that if a vote were held today in eastern Ontario whether we should wave a friendly goodbye to Quebec and thus restore some fairness in the federal public service close to 80 per cent would vote in favour. In fact I suspect that most of the 80 per cent would be happy to vote bye bye more than once if they could!

CHAPTER THIRTY-ONE

SAUCE FOR THE GOOSE SHOULD BE SAUCE FOR THE GANDER!

It's not just within the federal public service where a little fairness would be a good idea.

For years, trades people, truck drivers and construction workers in eastern Ontario have been screaming bloody murder over the fact that while Quebec workers and truck drivers flood into Ontario every day by the thousands, it's virtually impossible for anyone living in Ontario to be allowed to drive a nail in Quebec.

Labour mobility agreements, supposedly designed to insure that workers would not be impeded in any fashion by provincial borders were signed between Quebec and Ontario in 1993—1996 and yet again in 2006. Each time the story was always the same. Construction project parking lots in eastern Ontario were, and still are, a sea of Quebec license plates. Quebec construction project parking lots were, and still are, a sea of Quebec license plates.

No matter what agreements are signed; no matter what promises are made; no matter what assurances are provided it is always a one-way flow of traffic across the interprovincial bridges; Quebecers heading into Ontario in the morning with their lunch pails. Quebecers heading back into Quebec in the late afternoon with empty lunch pails.

Some of the worst examples of the blatant unfairness of the situation occurred during the construction of the huge National Archives Building in Gatineau and the Hull Casino. Ontario workers didn't get a sniff at either job, but Quebec workers by the hundreds swarmed over the Palladium building site (home to the Ottawa Senators) as it rose like a giant mushroom in the center of a weed filled farmer's field in Kanata.

Aside from Tim Hortons, it's doubtful any of them ever dropped a dime on the Ontario side!

The dispute became so heated at one point that Ontario truckers "accidentally" dumped an entire load of gravel on one of the interprovincial bridges, between Ottawa and Hull, greatly impeding the flow of traffic for most of the day.

The situation for Ontario truckers hasn't improved in the least despite all the agreements and promises. As one glaring example, during the cold and snowy winter of 2012/1013, the City of Ottawa continued to hire Quebec plated dump trucks to haul snow, while dozens of Ontario trucks with their drivers sat idle.

Several truckers phoned my show during that winter; so mad they threatened to shut down bridges again. None of Ottawa's City councillors nor the mayor seemed concerned enough about it to bother explaining or trying to put a stop to the blatant unfairness of it all.

The argument you sometimes hear is that we've got to hire Quebec workers because there aren't enough skilled tradesmen or even labourers on the Ontario side of the border doesn't hold water when it comes to truck drivers. The Greater Ottawa Truckers Association says their 160 members who collectively own about 600 dump trucks can handle all the work there is available on the Ontario side—even during heavy snowstorms. "We don't need Quebec trucks on this side of the Ottawa River," says Ron Barr, a spokesperson for the Association. "We have plenty of drivers and trucks to handle whatever needs to be done."

All the while of course, there is not a chance in Hell that either the Quebec provincial or municipal governments would be caught dead hiring an Ontario plated truck. In fact, according to more than one trucker who has called me, even an Ontario truck with all the proper licensing enters Quebec at great risk.

"I drive a brand new dump truck," explained one driver to me, "my company has it fully licensed to work in Quebec, but almost the moment I cross the bridge and enter that blessed province, there's someone there to pull me over and put me through every test known to mankind. In one month they had me at the side of the road three separate times. On another occasion they made me drive a good ten miles to a garage that supposedly checked my brakes and lights which of course were just fine."

"To be blunt about it," said this particular driver, "if you're an Ontario trucker in Quebec they treat you like a piece of dog dirt!"

Walter Parnic is unlikely to disagree with that assessment.

His electrical contracting company Power-Tek recently applied for a contract on the Quebec side but finally gave up after his staff spent more than 25 hours trying to "wiggle our way through the process."

All the documents, forms and regulations were in French only, then he was hit with a $750 dollar fee for membership in the Master Electricians of Quebec, plus a $154 contribution to its indemnity fund, then a $641 electrical contractors' license. According to Parnic, when they asked him, in addition to all the money, to hand over all copies of business licenses, master license, articles of incorporation, financial statements, and invoices for the past five years he finally packed in it.

"We got one third the way through the application," says Parnic when I said, "Stop, let's not take this any further, this is totally ridiculous! It's easier for me to get jobs in Poland than in Quebec!"

Parnic was in the spectators' gallery at Queen's Park in Toronto on May 29, 2013 when Progressive Conservative MPP Jack MacLaren (Carleton-Mississippi Mills) tabled a bill entitled "Fairness is a Two Way Street" which calls for a ban on Quebec workers coming into Ontario, until Ontario workers have equal opportunity in Quebec.

Actually the bill, which was greeted with catcalls and jeers by the Liberals and NDP, is identical legislation to the act that was passed by the Mike Harris government in 1999, but repealed by the McGuinty Liberals in 2006. Bill 80, as it was called, was defeated on September 12, 2013 when the Liberals and NDP voted againt it.

If it had passed the Bill would have forced construction contractors from Quebec to register with the Jobs Protection Office of Ontario before doing construction work or even submitting a bid for construction work in Ontario. It would also have barred Quebec companies from obtaining certificates, licenses or permits without proving they have registered with the Jobs Protection Office first.

It would have stated that Ontario's provincial government, municipalities and other public and boards would not be allowed to hire contractors from Quebec nor could construction companies sub-contract to another company that is based in or employs Quebec workers, until Ontario workers have the same rights to work in Quebec as Quebec workers have enjoyed for years.

In particular, the ban would apply to the giant multi billion-dollar light rail project started in early 2013 in Ottawa, a job that will employ, if the ban does not proceed, thousands of Quebecers from engineers to labourers.

The Bill provides fines of up to $25,000 for each day or part of a day that the corporation continues to work in contravention. Individual workers could be fined up to $2,000 per day if they ignore the rules.

The mere fact we need such a bill to protect Ontario workers is further evidence of the incredible pandering to Quebec that is still rampant!

You really have to ask yourself why anyone in Ontario would object to a bill that simply states that Ontario workers should have the same right to work in Quebec, as Quebec workers have to work in Ontario.

It should be obvious that until Quebec becomes a separate country this preferential treatment will continue unabated.

We have large numbers of people in the ROC who believe it is "progressive" to grant Quebec special privileges, turn a blind eye to blatant discrimination against Anglos, and to jeer and catcall those who advocate fair treatment for Ontario workers.

The left wing (progressives) believes that all minorities are by definition disadvantaged, discriminated against, victimized, oppressed, etc. This oppression, of course, is always at the hands of the "advantaged" majority, which in this case is those of us who have the "misfortune" of being raised in an English-speaking household. Thus the "progressives" believe that in order to balance the scales of justice all minorities must be provided preferential treatment, given special benefits, even their most heinous crimes must be viewed through a different lens.

French Canadians, according to the "progressives" are doubly deserving of preferential treatment. Not only are they a minority group, a little French puddle in the midst of a vast English sea, but they are only trying to preserve their language and culture. A noble people forced to defend themselves in whatever way possible against the raging English mob!

They believe allowing Quebecers to work in Ontario while denying that right to Ontarians in Quebec only helps to right the great injustice done to French Canada during and since the Plains of Abraham and anyone who doesn't agree with this analysis is not only wrong, but deeply in sin and probably even racist!

You may disagree with my assessment, but how else can you explain not only the situation involving workers—but also the very blatant and completely obvious preferential treatment that has been meted out to Quebec since the early 1960s?

CHAPTER THIRTY -TWO

THE COST!!!

And if Anglos being chased out of the public service and Ontario workers denied access to Quebec jobs don't convince you that perhaps the time has come to give Quebec a gentle little nudge out the door, then this chapter surely will. At the very least it may convince those of you who pay taxes in any form.

Because not only are we pumping truck loads of our hard earned tax dollars into Canada's bilingualism programs, but take a wild guess at who gets the nasty end of the stick?

Right on! You guessed right! Anglos in Quebec!

If there is a more graphic illustration of the blatant discrimination and mean spiritedness of Quebec towards its English-speaking minority than what I am about to reveal, again I ask that you call me.

According to The Fraser Institute, the total annual cost to Canadian taxpayers for federal and provincial spending on bilingualism is $2.4 billion. Please keep in mind that does not include spending by various municipalities. There doesn't appear to be any accurate accounting of what bilingualism costs our cities, towns and villages, but you can be sure it's in the tens of millions. (Somewhere between $100,000 and $200,000 for that lawsuit in Russell Township alone!).

But let's take the $2.4 billion figure and see where it's being spent.

According to the Fraser Report, the federal government spends $1.5 billion annually providing bilingual government services. The provinces, in addition, spend another $900 million for a total of $2.4 billion. That's $85 every year for every man, woman and child in the country.

Here are the figures that should have every Canadian up in arms demanding that Quebec either treat its minorities fairly or leave the Country!

Ontario pays $621 million annually for bilingual services for its Francophone minority. That's about 70 per cent of the total provincial costs of $900 million.

That works out to about $1,060 for every Francophone in the province.

In Alberta it's about $534 per Francophone.

Nova Scotia spends about $540 per Francophone.

In Manitoba the cost is about $410 per Francophone.

Saskatchewan spends $640 per Francophone.

In Prince Edward Island the figure is $946 per Francophone and Newfoundland and Labrador spends about $1,770 per Francophone.

You've missed Quebec you say. What is Quebec spending on bilingualism services for it English-speaking minority?

Glad you asked.

Remember, Ontario spends $621 million to provide bilingual services to its 583,000 Francophones—about $1,060 per Francophone.

Quebec with 575,000 English-speaking residents spends—ready for it—$50 million on bilingual services—just $85 per Anglo!

As the Toronto Sun said in a lead editorial (Jan. 19,2012), *"The reason for the discrepancy is that Ontario has spent decades building up educational language and cultural services for its Francophone minority, while Quebec has actively discouraged the use of English.*

Adds the Sun: *Whenever this discrepancy is pointed out, Quebec politicians of all stripes argue English speakers in Quebec are the "best treated minority in Canada."*

Apparently this means they're supposed to be grateful they're still allowed to use their own hospitals and schools, given the never-ending attacks on English mounted by various Quebec governments over the years.

But for Ontarians, the key issue is whether we're getting good value for tax money spent on bilingual services in our province. Until we force our politicians, of all stripes, to stop treating the subject like a politically correct sacred cow that can never be discussed without raising phony allegations of unfairness to Francophones, we'll never know.

~ • ~

So the next time Phil McNeely, the Language Commissioner, or anyone comes whining about the poor treatment of Francophones in any province, just remember the figures you've read here!

Not just Ontario, but all of Canada should be asking whether we are getting good value for the billions we spend on bilingualism. More importantly we should be asking ourselves exactly what is that we hope to achieve with our bilingualism policies.

CHAPTER THIRTY-THREE

THE GREAT FUZZY DREAM

I fully understand and very much appreciate the efforts of our Fathers of Confederation to create a nation in which our two founding cultures—French and English— would not only have equal rights, but could live side by side in peace and harmony. I also understand and appreciate the intent of those who drafted our language laws to insure that both languages have official status in our federal government and in our courts. Lofty and noble intentions all round.

But let's for a change set aside the sugar plumb dreams and best laid plans and deal with reality. Not what many of us hoped and worked for. Not what could or should have been. Let's deal with reality.

And reality is this. As Quebec becomes more and more entrenched in its unique French language and culture, the rest of Canada becomes more entrenched in multiculturalism and the English language. Like it or not, our two solitudes are drifting further and further apart—each side understanding less and less of the other. It's no one's fault. It's just the way it is and is probably unavoidable.

Let's confront a bit more reality. Despite the $2.4 billion we are spending on bilingual services every year, outside of Quebec, Canada has less official bilingualism today than it had a decade ago.

Please note I said official bilingualism, because as the latest Canadian census (2011) shows, the great dream of a French-English national destiny is being replaced by something very different.

Which presents us with a grand irony!

Because what we are seeing here is Pierre Trudeau's great dream of official French-English bilingualism being sabotaged by his great invention of Canadian style multiculturalism!

Despite the billions we have poured into bilingualism, the numerous French immersion classes we have subjected our children to, the anguish that daily bubbles up from language training in the public service, fewer and fewer Canadians outside Quebec are able to speak both of Canada's official languages.

CHAPTER THIRTY-FOUR

A NEW KIND OF BILINGUALISM!

There's a new form of bilingualism marching across the country, the fastest growing of which is—ready for this—English and Tagalog!

You heard right.

According to the 2011 census, the proportion of Canadians who speak English and another language other than French at home jumped to 11.5 percent in 2011 from 9.1 percent in 2006.

Astonishingly, this compares to only 3.7 percent who speak English and French in the home.

The number of people who reported speaking Tagalog, a Philippine-based language, and English in their homes increased the most (plus 64 percent) between 2006 and 2011.

Even more revealing is the fact that while the number of people speaking English and a language other than French is increasing dramatically, the number of people outside Quebec able to speak both English and French is declining. In fact the most recent census indicates that while official bilingualism increased slightly in Quebec between

2006 and 2011, it declined about half a percent age point in the ROC to under 9 per cent.

Even in officially bilingual New Brunswick the number of people who classify themselves as bilingual French and English decreased from 33.4 per cent in 2006 to 33.2 percent in 2011.

Just to clarify—while the census shows that only 3.7 per cent of Canadians speak both English and French in the home, slightly less than 9 per cent of Canadians outside Quebec consider themselves bilingual. It's a little confusing I know, but the overall message is very clear.

As more and more and more people from a myriad of other countries flood into Canada bringing with them more than 200 different languages, for most of those living outside Quebec the second language they learn is English.

Here are some numbers from the 2011 census that provide us with a graphic example of exactly what immigration is doing to Trudeau's dream of coast to coast French and English bilingualism.

As of 2010, 6.8 million Canadians (20.6 percent) reported a mother tongue other than English or French. About 4.7 million speak a language other than English or French most often at home (14.2 percent).

More than 200 mother tongues are spoken in Canada, though only 22 have more than 100,000 speakers in Canada.

The largest group is Punjabi at 460,000, followed by Chinese (unspecified) with 441,000, Spanish (439,000), Italian (438,000), German (430,000), Cantonese (389,000) Tagalog (384,000), Arabic (374,000) and Mandarin (255,000).

In Toronto, about 1.8 million people reported speaking an immigrant language most often at home, led by Cantonese (8.8 percent), Chinese (7 percent), Urdu (5.9 percent) and Tamil (5.7 percent).

In Montreal, more than 600,000 people reported speaking an immigrant language at home. Of these, 17 percent spoke Arabic, 15 percent spoke Spanish and 8 per cent Italian.

In Vancouver, 712,000 people reported speaking an immigrant language at home, led by Punjabi and Chinese languages.

In Ottawa-Gatineau, 114,000 people reported speaking an immigrant language at home. More than 85 percent of these lived in Ontario. Arabic (20 percent), Spanish (8 percent) and Chinese (7 percent) were the leading languages.

But perhaps nothing more clearly indicates the declining status of French-English bilingualism than a statement by Jean-Pierre Corbeil, a language specialist at Statistics Canada who says a new study shows that since 1996, the percentage of 15 to 19 year olds outside Quebec who can converse in French has declined to 11.4% from 15.2%.

So much for the billions we spend on French immersion in our schools!

By now it should be clear that the fuzzy and very noble dream of creating a totally bilingual country where every citizen could easily and delightfully switch back and forth between French and English at the drop of a verb was always just that—a fuzzy but impossible dream.

There was a time when half the parents in the land insisted that their kids take French courses in elementary and secondary schools. Sorry, but unless you live in Quebec, even after eight or ten years of classroom instruction you will have difficulty ordering a pizza in French. I've made this claim on several occasions during my show and was always confronted by someone who claimed they had learned nearly perfect French in an Ontario or Alberta high school. My challenge was always the same. Okay—I'm a tourist just arrived in Canada from France and don't speak a word of English. Give me directions to the train station.

Sadly with rare exception the caller had great difficulty explaining in French how to flush the hotel toilet!

The exception is Quebec, where in addition to what is taught in school, you're surrounded by the French fact and pretty well forced to speak the language in order to just figure out the traffic signs!

But despite the number of parents packing their kids off to French immersion classes and all our other attempts at creating this wonderland of bilingualism, let's just tell the truth here. Let's have a long hard look at a fact we all know but seem to have great difficulty accepting.

That fact is: **QUEBEC IS FRENCH! THE REST OF THE COUNTRY IS ENGLISH!**

Over simplification? A bit. But not much. Yes, almost everyone in Quebec can speak at least a bit of English, but if you are going to live and work in that province you've got to speak French. With very rare exception everyone in Quebec can speak French and does so on a daily basis.

And sure a lot of people in New Brunswick are perfectly bilingual (about 34 percent), but that just backs up what I am saying. With very rare exception everyone in officially bilingual New Brunswick can speak English.

The same holds true of those other parts of Canada with substantial Francophone populations. There are lots of people who speak French in eastern Ontario, but you are very hard pressed to find any of them who don't speak English very well. Ditto places like Sudbury in northern Ontario, St. Boniface, Manitoba and every other Francophone enclave in the ROC.

Why is it so difficult for us to face the truth?

At least Quebec is honest about it. It boasts about the fact they have only one official language and spends almost nothing providing services in any other language. As I pointed out earlier, every year while good old Ontario spends more than $1,000 per Francophone on bilingual services, Quebec spends $85 and very shortly will spend even less.

What Quebec is saying is look. This is a French speaking province and we're going to become even more so, therefore don't come here thinking we're going to do anything to encourage you or help you to speak English. There is only one official language here and by the way we're not multicultural either!

Don't get me wrong; the majority of Quebecers today can speak English with some degree of fluency. They know they have to in order to compete in a global marketplace, but that doesn't change the fact that at home, in Quebec, they are going to speak French and if you want to live in Quebec you'd better learn to speak the language damn fast!

CHAPTER THIRTY-FIVE

WHY ARE WE DOING IT?

So now comes the question.

If Quebec wants no part of bilingualism why are we spending billions providing bilingual services to the rest of the country, especially since the rate of official bilingualism outside Quebec is declining?

Well, some will say, no matter what Quebec does, we in the rest of Canada must provide bilingual services because there are plenty of Francophones in other parts of the country.

Okay, but once again, let's be brutally frank.

Everyone who lives outside Quebec, even in those few predominately Francophone areas of Ontario and Manitoba, speaks English. They've got to and furthermore they know it.

It really is as simple as this. If you live in Quebec you're going to have to learn to speak French. If you live in any other province, with the possible exception of New Brunswick you're going to have to learn to speak English.

It is true, as we have already pointed out that we have immigrant populations that have not as yet acquired proficient English, but that's another story that has nothing to do with our two official languages. And for certain no one is suggesting or insisting that we acquire Mandarin or Farsi in order to service newcomers to Canada in the language of their choice.

So you really have to ask yourself why we are spending billions to provide French language services to people who understand English perfectly well? More specifically, why did we set out to do this?

I know the answer, because I was around and interviewed most of those involved when Lester Pearson launched his famous B and B Commission (Bilingualism and Biculturalism) and I was around and interviewed those responsible for all versions of the Official Languages Act and our Charter of Rights and Freedoms.

Very few of those I spoke with would come right out and admit it, but there was no question the primary purpose of our bilingualism policies was to appease Quebec. Or as it was explained to my listeners and me on many occasions by Prime Minister Pearson and others, "We want Quebecers to feel that all of Canada is their country. That no matter where they go they will feel welcome knowing that their language and culture are flourishing everywhere in Canada and most of all we want to insure that Canadians of both our founding cultures know that their federal government can speak to them on any matter in the language of their choice."

Unspoken at the time but hovering over this, like the sword of Damocles, was the growing separatist movement, the birth of the Parti Quebecois and FLQ bombings, the most dramatic of which was an attack on the Montreal Stock Exchange on February 13, 1969 injuring 27 people even as the Official Languages Act was being debated in Parliament.

It was hoped, if not expected, that the concessions made to Quebec and Francophones across the country would pull the rug out from under the feet of the nationalist movement and perhaps just as importantly, assure the continued domination of the Liberal Party in Quebec.

Obviously it didn't work.

What followed only months after the Act was passed was the 1970 October crisis during which British Trade Commissioner James Cross was kidnapped, Deputy Premier Pierre Laporte was brutally murdered by members of the FLQ and Trudeau said "just watch me" as he sent troops into the streets.

And, far from assuring continued Liberal victories, the Parti Quebecois garnered 24% of the popular vote in April of 1970, then with Rene Levesque at the helm, the separatists won the election in 1976 and the great Anglo exodus began in earnest!

CHAPTER THIRTY-SIX

ONLY QUEBECERS COUNT!

There's one more fact that seems difficult for many to absorb. Mark this down on your calendar! Hardly anyone in Quebec gives a sweet flying fox fart about the fate of Francophones outside their province.

There has been an assumption, naive as it is, that if we treat Francophones in the ROC really, really nice, provide French language government services, French language education where numbers warrant, expand bilingualism in our provincial and municipal governments, if we do all of that and more, then Quebec Francophones will be so grateful they will stop all this separatism business and treat their Anglophone minority a bit better!

Good luck with that!

Do you really think the average Quebecer cares if signs in Russell Township are in both languages?

Do you think the average Quebecer spends a single moment applauding Sudbury City Council for providing French language services in its hospitals?

Did the City of Ottawa get a gold star on the good-guy board for spending millions on bilingual services? ($1,778,912 just for translation services in 2012!)

Did anybody in Quebec stand up and cheer when Canada Post declared that all postmasters in the National Capital region must be bilingual?

Does the average Quebecois appreciate the fact that Vancouver has French language radio and TV?

Do they even know, let alone care in Quebec that St. Boniface has French language institutions including hospitals? Would most Quebecers even know where St. Boniface is?

Ever hear a word of thanks to the tens of thousands of parents across this land that took a big chunk of their hard earned money to send their children to French language schools?

You never did hear thanks Canada and you never will. For one simple fact. No matter the language you speak, the culture you adhere to. No matter where your heart may be, once you leave Quebec you are no longer a Quebecer and whether you speak French, Greek, English or Punjabi what happens to you is of little, if any, concern to the average Quebecois.

We've got to face the fact that no matter how well we treat Francophones in the ROC, it has no bearing on the way most Quebecers view Canada and plays no role in influencing the way Quebec treats Anglos.

That having been said, I don't think we can be too critical of Quebec in this regard since I see very little evidence that Anglos in the ROC are any more concerned about their English brothers and sisters in Quebec than Quebec is about their French brothers and sisters in the rest of the country. Let's be very honest here. If the ROC was all that concerned about the treatment of the English minority in Quebec we would have put a stop to it long ago.

I know this will tick a lot of you off, but the grim fact is, there was barely a peep of protest from across the land when more than a quarter million Anglos fled the discrimination and racism that became epidemic in Quebec.

In fairness, at the time, we Canadians were inundated with assurances by our political leaders, our media and the left wing that we mustn't be too critical of Quebec because they only were doing what they had to in order to preserve their language and culture.

Yes, I freely admit it, for a while I was part of that media persuasion team! That was then! This is now!

Anyone the least bit critical of what was happening in Quebec was quickly dumped into the nearest dustbin and pelted with accusations of racism, knuckle dragging, drooling and farting beneath the sheets! You get the idea!

I certainly learned my lesson. There was a time when CTV's Sunday Edition with Mike Duffy, Mike Harris, Barbara Yaffe, Lowell Green and a weekly guest was one of the most viewed television shows in the country. It came to an abrupt halt not long after my on-air confrontation with a leading Quebec separatist during which I blamed racist policies for the mass exodus of Anglos from her province. It was all too much, apparently for the dear folk and gentle people who, at the time, made up the rules at CTV. In a panic they pulled the plug on me and shortly after that, the entire show.

I suspect that if that episode occurred in more recent times, it wouldn't have caused even a mild gas pain amongst the most delicate of sensibilities. Times have changed that much!

The question is still there though isn't it?

If all Francophones in the ROC speak English; if Quebecers could not care less about how we treat their French-speaking cousins outside La Belle Province, exactly why are we spending billions trying to teach Anglos how to speak French?

It's not as though Francophones in the ROC are especially appreciative of our efforts to accommodate them and their language. You can hardly turn around these days without another complaint being launched about the lack of French something or other.

We've already talked about the Russell Township sign war, Cornwall is deeply divided over French only hospitals and clinics and now we've got a Francophone couple taking their 7-UP case to the Supreme Court.

Back in 2009, Michel and Lynda Thibodeau launched eight complaints about lack of French language service aboard Air Canada flights. One of the complaints was that they couldn't order a 7-UP in French. They sued for more than half a million dollars and incredibly the Federal Court awarded them $12,000. The judge ruled, "The violation of their rights caused them a moral prejudice, pain and suffering and loss of enjoyment of their vacation". (No, I'm not making this up!) The Federal Court of Appeal subsequently reduced the $12,000 settlement to a bit over $5,000.

Undaunted the couple took the case to the Supreme Court of Canada and even more unbelievably, the Supreme Court has agreed to hear the case! (Can't someone find a real job for these black-robed birds?)

Think of it. More than 280 thousand Anglos pack up all their processions and flee discrimination in Quebec with hardly a peep of protest, but the Supreme Court decides to take the case of a couple obviously devastated because they have trouble ordering a 7-UP in French!

And you still wonder why I think the time has come to ask Quebec for a nice friendly divorce!

CHAPTER THIRTY-SEVEN

THE VELVET DIVORCE

I have no idea how the Slovakian army would acquit itself in a fox hunt let alone any kind of fire-fight, but I can tell you this, there is no army in the world capable of doing a better job of rifle acrobatics performed to the beat of rock and roll.

Whether the performance that sunny afternoon in the town square in Bratislava was part of Slovak army training or strictly for the tourists pouring off the riverboats I have no idea. But it was fascinating. None of us had ever seen anything like it before. Picture a smartly dressed corps of about 50 soldiers tossing their rifles into the air like batons, spinning them around their bodies, flipping them back and forth, up and down the ranks, snapping them to the ground with nary a fumble, all to the beat of a military band pounding out a vigorous "Eye of the Tiger".

One of our shipmates, a history professor from Toronto, had warned us that we'd find that things were pretty grim in Slovakia. "The economy has been in the dumper since they separated from the Czech Republic back in 1993," he told us. "Think Quebec 15 or so years after separation and that's pretty well what you'll see today in Slovakia."

He went on to claim that if given the chance he believed at least 90 per cent of Slovakians would vote to rejoin with the Czech Republic. He wasn't so sure of Czech sentiment.

But as it turns out, when it comes to Slovakia our professor friend was just slightly misinformed. (A condition epidemic in his profession!)

What we found in Bratislava, following the spinning rifle show, was a thriving and thoroughly captivating little city of about half a million people, filled with historic sites, monuments, museums, theatres and no fewer than three universities. The streets were lined with restaurants, the outdoor cafes filled with people at all hours of the day.

The nearby VW plant, we were informed by our tour guide, was running two shifts and trying to hire skilled tradesmen from nearby Hungary. As the republic's capital, government, as in Ottawa, was a major employer and highly lucrative.

A day long visit is a poor indicator of a country's economic health, but all 23 members of out little group, reported the same thing: Everyone they talked with, in their meanders through town, from cab drivers, to waitresses to store keepers and even in a couple cases café patrons seemed reasonably prosperous and happy with the way things had worked out since parting company with the Czechs.

There didn't seem to be any animosity. In fact when I asked a couple people we met in a local restaurant if they would like to rejoin the Czech Republic they seemed puzzled by the question.

When I suggested to our professor friend that if Quebecers were to see how well Slovakia has done since separation it would probably change a lot of minds and have separatists jumping for joy, he had to nod his head in agreement.

Interestingly enough, the Financial Post reported early in 2013 that the Slovakian economy was one of the strongest of all small European countries, so our tourist observations from two years earlier were obviously not entirely out of whack.

The pro-business reforms implemented by the Slovakian government paved the way for Slovakia to join the Euro Zone in 2009.

While growth dropped from double-digit pre-European crisis highs to negative territory in 2009, it swiftly rebounded to an average growth rate of over three per cent in 2010-2012. Slovakia's banking system remains sound and it is expected that the country will be out of a deficit position possibly as early as 2014—far sooner than most western nations, including Canada.

And please keep in mind the fact that Slovakia has managed all of this without Quebec's 46 billion barrels of oil and trillions of cubic feet of natural gas bubbling beneath their feet!

What's particularly fascinating about what is called the "Velvet Divorce" between the Czech Republic and Slovakia are the similarities we find here in Canada. All polls prior to the breakup of Czechoslovakia showed little support for separation. As with the situation here the big fear was economic.

Most European professors and other assorted "experts" predicted financial catastrophe, especially for the much smaller Slovakia.

Obviously many factors were involved in the decision to go their separate ways. Just as is the case with Quebec and the rest of Canada the Czech and Slovak populations had been slowly drifting apart for many years and with the fall of communism and the formation of a newly democratic Czechoslovakia, disputes broke out during the creation of a new Constitution. (Here in Canada Quebec still hasn't even signed on to our Constitution!)

There were major disagreements over fiscal and cultural policies. Many Czechs believed that the Slovaks held a disproportionate amount of power that was holding the entire country back. (Sound familiar?)

Just as here in Canada, one of the main bones of contention was the fact that Czechoslovakian version of equalization payments meant that the Czechs were required to pump substantial amounts of money into what is now Slovakia. (Eerie isn't it?)

Halting equalization payments played a major role in the decision to separate, just as it doubtless would here in Canada.

Amazingly enough, despite the general antipathy to separation, the multitude of difficult problems to be resolved and the fear of a financial disaster, the decision to separate and the subsequent negotiations were remarkably tranquil. The national debt was divided up in proportion to population. The Czech Republic has about twice the population of Slovakia, so the Czech's assumed the largest part of the debt at a ratio of roughly two to one.

Just as we would have to do here in Canada with Quebec separation countless decisions had to be made concerning everything from ownership of government buildings to federal boundaries. In some cases today you will find the Czech Republic on one side of the street— Slovakia on the other. You can imagine the difficulties!

The negotiations were completed in less than six months with such goodwill on both sides that at midnight December 31, 1992 there were handshakes all round and what to this day is called the velvet divorce was complete. Czechoslovakia ceased to exist.

Replaced on January 1, 1993 by two good-friend nations—the Czech Republic and Slovakia—both of which, some 20 years later, are doing just fine, thank you very much!

It is true that for the first few years after separation the Slovakian economy did suffer, but independence seemed to somehow energize the citizens until today their per capita GDP rivals that of France and is superior to that of either Spain or Italy. Both the Czech and Slovakian economies have escaped the financial crisis that continues to plague much of Europe, although strangely enough it is the Czech Republic that seems to be in more financial difficulty today than Slovakia.

Could we accomplish the same thing here in Canada with as much good will as they did along the banks of the Danube? Why not? Are we Canadians not as civil as Europeans? Are our negotiating skills any less? Our goodwill inferior? I think not!

They claim that the residents of the Czech Republic and Slovakia are better friends today after the divorce than they ever were when together. Could that happen here in Canada?

Why not?

Over there they call it the velvet divorce. Even gentler to the touch is a beaver pelt!

CHAPTER THIRTY-EIGHT

WHERE ARE THE SEPARATISTS?

Some pundits and others supposedly in the know claim that the appetite for separation is moribund in Quebec. They point to recent polls as proof of this. Don't for one moment believe it. How many of those getting dandy little Canadian pay cheques, as NDP MPs are nothing but separatists in disguise? More to the point, how many separatists would there be if we ever stopped propping up their social programs with about $9 billion a year in transfer payments from the rest of Canada?

One of the reasons that support for independence appears to be low is the fact that today Quebecers essentially have the best of two worlds. Why cut yourself off from billions of dollars from Canada when you've got almost everything you want without actually signing the divorce papers?

To a large degree Quebec is already a separate nation. Its provincial legislature is the National Assembly; it controls its own immigration policy; incredibly Quebec even has its own Ministry of International Relations (Ministere de Relations Internationales) which oversees a network of, at last count, 22 foreign delegations, 10 foreign bureaus and four foreign trade offices. For years the province has frequently bypassed the federal government in dealing directly with foreign nations on matters other than trade. Ask anyone in Ottawa who's honest and they will tell you that Quebec probably has closer ties to France and other nations in the Francophonie than does the federal government.

As with all other provinces, of course, Quebec is fully in charge of education, including universities and colleges, healthcare, welfare and almost all social programs. It surely begs the question; aside from national defense and a few other things like broadcast policy, exactly what role does the federal government play in the life of the average Quebecer?

The answer to that question is—-not a heck of a lot, except of course, keep those Canadian dollars pouring in!

Holy smokes, Radio Canada is now talking about removing the word Canada and calling itself ICI instead! (An idea now on the back burner). Apparently however, they will still accept the billion plus dollars that Canada pays out to keep the CBC afloat!

And as this column published in the April 2, 2013 edition of the Sherbrooke Record newspaper attests, not all the separatists are Francophones and not all the impetus for separation stems from cultural or language concerns or demands.

ENGLISH, EDUCATED AND SEPARATIST!

A few weeks ago, politically active students at the Universite de Sherbrooke organized a Sovereignty Week during which the Record met and interviewed three students—Colleen McCool, Emma Callas, and James McDonald.

The three are part of a small and perhaps surprising demographic; they are young educated, English and sovereignists.

So what makes separation such an attractive option?

What kind of personal experience leads a young, educated, English speaking Quebecer to espouse sovereignty?

Colleen McCool grew up in Montreal, where from grade three to the end of high school she studied in French at an alternative school. She then attended an English CEGEP before opting to pursue a degree in political science at the Universite de Sherbrooke.

"I chose Sherbrooke," she explains, "because I wanted to improve my written French and also because I wanted to see how comfortable I'd feel in Quebec outside the City of Montreal.

"It's been a bit of a mixed bag," she continues. "Generally, people have been generous and accommodating, but sometimes I've also felt a sense of wariness or mistrust."

Emma Callas, who is in her second year in the Faculty of Law, was a little reluctant to have her name in the paper. "My immediate family is neutral on the issue of separation, but my extended family and family friends are federalist. As well, most law firms in Quebec are not pro-sovereignty and I'll be applying for a job in few years!" Nevertheless, the West Island native (born of Greek parents) agreed to be interviewed.

Emma attended French elementary and high schools where she remembers being reprimanded for speaking English on the playground. "I'd get a figurative slap on the wrist for talking English with my English friends," she says, "but nobody got upset with me for talking Greek with my Greek friends." After high school she went to Marianopolis, a private English CEGEP and then to McGill where she studied economics and political science.

James McDonald was born in Germany; his mother is American and his father a Montreal born Canadian. James did most of his schooling in the United States. When he was 21 he moved to Chicoutimi with the intention of studying French for a few months. He ended up earning a B.A. at the Universite de Quebec a Chicoutimi where he studied political science, English and communications. He's now in his second year at the Universite de Sherbrooke.

Ironically, it wasn't living in the independantise Saguenay that swayed James to separatism, but rather living in the heart of Canada in Waterloo, Ontario.

"When I decided to come to Canada seven years ago," says James, "it was because the image I'd formed of it was based on the notion that Canada was a bilingual and bicultural country. The three years I lived in Chicoutimi, I was a federalist. My experience was that when you live in French both the federalist and separatist options are possible. Everybody can talk about it and it doesn't matter if you're for or against, or undecided, because there are lots of people in all three camps."

"I find it different when I'm with an English speaking group," he continues. "It's as if there's denial that a separatist option could exist. Federalism for them is an emotional issue."

When I took a job in Ontario, I went with the feeling that, with my facility in both French and English, that I was fully Canadian. That wasn't the case. What I found was that French was not seen as a positive. Both in the print media, like the National Post and Maclean's and in daily conversation there was often—too often—some form of Quebec bashing," he says.

"I eventually came to reject federalism," he adds, "because there isn't any kind of linguistic equality. I'm convinced that there is no bright future for the French language in Canada, including Quebec, if Quebec remains a province."

For Emma, the drift towards a pro-sovereignty position came gradually and began with a loss of faith in the federalist model. "As I see it, federalism in Canada simply does not work," she says. "You can't have someone in British Columbia, for example, making decisions for someone living in say, Nova Scotia. I believe in the principle that what can be done locally, should be done locally. It's a principle used by the Supreme Court to distinguish between provincial and federal jurisdiction."

"I find the image of an island of French in a sea of English very appealing," she adds. "I can understand wanting to protect and promote the French language. The challenge for the separatist side is to make it clear that protecting French is not equivalent to attacking English. It's only in the last several months that I've come to be pro-sovereignty."

For Colleen McCool, the question is still up in the air. "Both my parents are English-speaking," she points out, "but my father, in particular, has always shown a lot of respect for the French language and for the sovereignty cause, even though he is not pro-sovereignty. In some ways, I've been considering the question since I was 12 or 13 when I first started becoming aware of it. I've become more open to the idea of separation since coming to Sherbrooke, but at this point I'm still on the fence. I just don't know which side I'm really on."

She knows she's not alone. Shortly after the Conservatives won the last election," she says, " a friend of the family, who is a staunch federalist, commented that the policies of Stephen Harper could lead him to seriously consider separatism."

"If you can step back from the emotional aspect and look at it logically and rationally," says Emma, "separatism makes sense."

Quebec has already been recognized both as a distinct society and as a nation," James points out. 'There's no doubt in my mind that Quebec has much to offer on the international stage, particularly in terms of environmental and educational issues. I don't think there's anywhere else where I could study law for $3000 a year. I certainly could never afford to become a lawyer if I were in the States."

"Quebec is a much more progressive society than the rest of Canada when it comes to women's rights," says Colleen.

Emma agrees. "Quebec is more liberal and progressive in lots of other ways as well," says Emma. "Quebec's attitude is different on at least half a dozen topics: The legalization of marijuana, the acceptance of homosexuality, the question of euthanasia, prostitution, the rehabilitation of convicted criminals—Quebec believes that someone who has committed a crime can be helped to lead a productive life. Harper is completely bent on incarceration."

"Quebec," James says, "generally has a live and let live attitude. It's essentially a pacifist nation, much more pro-peace than pro-war. There isn't much enthusiasm in Quebec for Harper's plan to spend $35 billion on fighter jets."

As for being an English-speaking citizen in a predominately French culture, all three consider it a positive and feel in no way threatened.

~ • ~

(Apparently it never dawned on any of these students that their $3 thousand university annual tuition is largely thanks to the $9 billion of so sucked out of the rest of Canada, mostly from those bloody capitalists in Alberta and Saskatchewan! Oh well, no one ever said higher education was perfect!)

CHAPTER THIRTY-NINE

THE REAL QUESTION!

But the real question today is not how many separatists or soft nationalists or wavering separatists or dipping toes into separatist waters separatists or separatists just for the hell of it or separatists to spite mommy and daddy there are in Quebec.

The real question, and so far I seem to be the only one with the guts to ask it is:

HOW MANY SEPARATISTS ARE THERE
IN THE REST OF CANADA?

Forget a referendum or polling in Quebec. They've already had two chances at that! How about a chance for the rest of us to have a say?

What do you suppose the results would be if any polling outfit had the courage to ask one of these questions of those of us who do not live in La Belle Province?

How about this for a question for the ROC?

Does your Canada still include Quebec?"

Or how about:

"Do you support giving Quebec a friendly little push out of the Country?"

Or:

"Do you support creating a Canada separate and independent from the province of Quebec?"

I think you get the point!

We can only speculate as to the findings of any such polling but the results would be very interesting would they not? If the response from my listeners, not just during my recent polling, but also for the past several years is any indication, at least a slim majority would vote to bid adieu to the land of the fleur de lis! How would you vote?

But can there be any doubt whatsoever how Canadians would respond if asked this question:

Has the time come for the rest of Canada to stop pumping nearly nine billion dollars a year into Quebec?

I'd do a headstand on the Sparks Street Mall or downtown Yonge Street, if you wish, if the "yes" vote on a question of that nature wouldn't be overwhelming. Especially if voters read the following chapter!

CHAPTER FORTY

THE GREAT EQUALIZATION CON GAME!

During the six years between the fiscal years 2005/2006 and 2011/2012 a total of $91,709,000,000 was transferred from the federal government to various provinces under Canada's equalization payment program. Yes that's $91 billion, 709 million! Of that amount, Quebec received $50,071,000,000. Yes that's $50 billion 71 million!

To clarify even further, of the more than $91 billion dollars transferred to provinces during a six-year period ending in 2012, Quebec received more than half—more than fifty billion dollars!

During those six years, all provinces except for Alberta received at least some of the money, but as of the last two or possibly three years, three of those recipient provinces, (B.C., Saskatchewan and Newfoundland/Labrador) have turned their economies around and are now contributing to the other six.

This means that Quebec today is receiving an even larger share of the economic pie than ever before and shows no signs of attempting to become a "have" province. (Why bother working, when others will feed you? Why bother tapping into your own oil and gas reserves, when you can get Alberta to pay for what you need?)

In fairness, on a per capita basis Manitoba, New Brunswick and P.E.I receive more in the way of transfer payments than Quebec, but the fact remains that after some 50 years of massive subsidies totaling hundreds of billions of dollars, Quebec has not improved its financial performance in relation to other provinces and is actually further from so called "have" status than at any time in the past 30 years.

Much of the blame for this can be attributed directly to, as the Globe and Mail once described it, Quebec's "separatist adventures" that have been well documented, but it is also true that the province has deliberately refused to harvest many of its vast reserves of natural resources, in particular oil and natural gas.

In February of 2013 the Parti Quebecois government imposed a five-year moratorium on oil and shale-gas development along the St. Lawrence River—a staggering blow to the economy. (Quebec announced on June 6, 2013 that it would allow some exploratory drilling on Anticosti Island. Since exploration has already indicated the vast resources available, exploratory drilling is just a stall tactic)

While the Quebec Oil and Gas Association has refused comment on the moratorium for obvious political reasons, they don't deny that there are sufficient supplies of shale gas and oil along the St. Lawrence and on Anticosti Island to supply all of the Province's domestic requirements for generations to come.

It is estimated that today Quebec consumes about $2 billion a year of natural gas, all of it imported. Tapping into the province's gas, without even touching the vast supplies of oil believed to be beneath the surface would save the province all of that $2 billion.

The area called Old Harry, located on the northern-most island of the Magdalene Islands has twice the potential of the Hibernia Oil Field off the coast of Newfoundland. Old Harry has been found to contain at least two billion barrels of recoverable oil and up to five trillion cubic feet of recoverable gas. Oil actually seeps up through the earth's crust into the ocean. The area is about 29 kilometers long, straddling the Quebec-Newfoundland boundary.

This refusal to stand up to the environmentalists, or more probably their reluctance to share the riches with all of Canada and tap into the enormous wealth that lies just beneath the surface of the province and become much more self-sufficient is not a new phenomenon.

Perhaps the best illustration of this is a column that appeared on Brian Lilly's website on April 26th, 2012, written by Eric Duhaime, a highly respected columnist for Journal de Montreal, the National Post and the Sun News chain.

Entitled: **DRILL, BABY, DRILL!** Duhaime writes:

If Quebecers are sincere and want to stop depending so much on the transfer payments from Canada's richest provinces, they could just start doing what Alberta, Saskatchewan and Newfoundland—the three richest provinces in the country—are doing and say yes to homemade oil.

Even if most governments in the western world seem obsessed with the idea of adopting cost-ineffective programs to promote so called green energy sources, like it or not, oil remains the main and most viable resource. Over the past 20 years, our oil consumption has increased. Oil will still be the largest source of primary energy in the world for at least the next few decades. This will remain the case until renewable energies become less expensive.

In the meantime, somebody, somewhere needs to extract, refine and sell "dirty" oil. It's a matter of survival, not just for our cars and trucks, but also for heating, fertilizers, pesticides, synthetic fibers, plastics, solvents, paints, rubber, detergents, cosmetics, medicine and so on.

The most prosperous provinces in Canada and the wealthiest American states are those exploiting their oil and natural gas resources.

Some other "have not" provinces also have great oil potential but do not exploit it. Quebec is one example.

The Montreal Economic Institute (MEI) published a relevant study by Prof. Germain Belzile, entitled, "The benefit of oil production development in Quebec." According to several evaluations, there are more than 46 billion barrels of oil in two locations in Quebec—Anticosti Island and Old Harry.

The MEI conservatively estimates that at $100 a barrel, and assuming that just one tenth of those reserves were recoverable, Quebec's potential production worth would be more than $400 billion. And we are not even talking here about the other great unexploited natural resources reserves that Quebec refuses to exploit—shale gas.

What would happen if Quebec gave a green light to oil development?

"Obviously, the Quebec government would receive royalties, but it would also receive tax revenue from the private income generated by higher growth. This would allow the government to reduce the tax burdens of households and businesses and might even help it pay back a part of its public debt and escape from its dependence on transfers from the federal equalization program," Belzile informs us.

For the tree-huggers, we can all that we would take greater care of the environment since we would not need to carry oil from the other end of Canada, or even worse from the Middle East.

Alberta's average household income in 2009 was $71,000, compared to $50,600 in Quebec. La Belle Province will not become more "belle" or narrow the gap by depending more and more on its neighbour's wallet and work.

Quebec's economic problems have, in fact, nothing to do with the fiscal imbalance of federalism, as separatists claim, but have everything to do with its energy and environmental policies.

Instead of screaming and begging for more money from Ottawa and Alberta, why don't Quebecers roll up their sleeves and start digging for the wealth sitting underneath their feet. Drill, Quebec, drill!

~ • ~

CHAPTER FORTY-ONE

CONCENTRATED STUPIDITY AND COWARDICE

Eric's sentiments are shared by many in Quebec, except, sadly, those in government who are now even opposed to allowing Alberta oil to flow through pipelines to refineries in Quebec and New Brunswick.

As just one example of how Quebec continues to turn its back on self-sufficiency consider this. Texas-based Valero Energy Corp says it is prepared to invest as much as $200 million in its Quebec refinery if the government will allow Enbridge to proceed with its plan to reverse its Line 9 pipeline allowing western Canadian oil to flow eastward from Sarnia to Montreal. The company would then transport the oil by ship up the St. Lawrence to the Valero refinery near Quebec City. In addition, Valero wants to carry additional oil from Sarnia to its Quebec City refinery by rail.

TransCanada Corp. also has plans to construct a new pipeline bringing Alberta oil to eastern Canada refineries, including the Suncor refinery in Montreal, the Valero refinery and the Irving refinery in St. John.

All of this however requires approval from the Quebec government that has imposed a five-year moratorium on fracking for oil and gas and is dragging its feet on approving construction of new pipelines or even reversing the flow of the Line 9 pipeline.

Despite suspicions that Quebec's refusal to harvest the vast reserves of oil and gas are a ploy to avoid sharing the wealth with the ROC, the Marois government continues to maintain that it is for environmental reasons that they refuse to drill.

There is no question that the tiny but obviously very influential environmental movement has convinced many Quebecers that it somehow damages the planet more to take oil and gas from the ground beneath your feet than it does to pump it out of the ground in some middle eastern Sheikdom, load it aboard giant ships, transport it across the Atlantic, transfer it into trucks for shipment to refineries where, finally as gasoline and other products it is loaded aboard more trucks or railcars and delivered to the pumps and stores.

It's fascinating to note that many of the leading environmentalists are women who obviously see nothing wrong with fattening the pockets of sheiks who deny women even basic rights. Every dollar spent on Middle Eastern oil rather than domestic is one more dollar to despots who in some cases finance terrorism, deny women the right to leave their homes unaccompanied by a male and have their wives whipped for showing an ankle.

The hypocrisy is nothing short of astonishing!

As recently as mid-May of 2013, Francoise Bertrand, President and CEO of the Federation of Quebec Chambers of Commerce said that "moratoriums and new regulations are sending a signal to the investment community to take their business elsewhere."

"We are very concerned about the energy policy in Quebec," said Mr. Bertrand. "Already five Quebec refineries have closed down in the past 30 years and Shell shuttered its 161,000 barrels-per-day Montreal refinery two years ago."

And consider this. Even as it sits on some 46 billion barrels of oil, and trillions of cubic feet of natural gas—even as it drags its feet approving pipelines—this year Quebec will spend about $16 billion on imported oil plus the $2 billion on imported natural gas!

As further evidence of just how earth shatteringly stupid is Quebec's reluctance to tap into its tremendous reserves of oil and gas shake your head at this. Hundreds of billions of dollars worth of oil and gas are close to the surface of Anticosti Island which, according to the 2006 census has a population of 281, most of whom eek out a meager existence fishing.

Come on Quebec! Sink a few oil wells and instead of making trillionaires out of Arab Sheiks make instant millionaires out of every island resident, man, woman and child for heaven sakes.

Your reluctant decision in June of 2013 to allow "some exploratory drilling" on Anticosti, is according to observers, just a stalling tactic. The exploration has already been done, the incredible reserves have been found and all that prevents actually drilling for black gold is government approval.

Why in the world is the Quebec government bound and determined to pour tens of billions of dollars into the Middle East, but not into the pockets of their own people?

I repeat, either persuading or forcing Quebec to become independent would compel them to use common sense, stop the foot dragging and launch them into self-sufficiency. Not having the ROC to fund their seven dollar daycare, their almost free university tuition and other social programs would send the government scrambling to see how fast they could yank some of that black gold out of the rocky soil, besides which they understand only too well that independence means not sharing the wealth!

What Duhaime doesn't say but easily could, is that if Quebec were to drill, baby drill for the wealth beneath their feet, not only could they easily become a "have" province and stop the drain on the rest of the country, but and this is vital to my argument.

With 46 billion barrels of oil and a virtual endless supply of shale gas, the Republic of Quebec could do very well on its own, thank you very much!

Oil and all the jobs and wealth it creates has converted Newfoundland from a "have not" province with one of the lowest standards of living and the highest unemployment rate in the country into a "have" province with a booming economy. Quebec has far more oil and gas at its disposal than Newfoundland but rather than drilling and or fracking for it, the Quebec government chooses instead to play the poor sister of Confederation and demand and receive more and more welfare, ironically most of it from the proceeds of oil pumped from Alberta soil.

With this knowledge, all arguments about Quebec not having the ability to stand on its own feet are shot down. Not only could it easily stand on its own two feet, but with the billions already pouring into the province from the James Bay Hydro electric project plus the billions more ready to be pumped from the ground, Quebec could easily become the richest province in Canada, or as an independent nation—one of the richest countries in the world!

Very clearly it's not their feet that pose the problem—it's their heads!!

And of course there is another question in the minds of many.

Could the Lac Megantic tragedy have been avoided if Quebec had adopted a different stance regarding pipelines?

We will never know of course, but this we do know. There is absolutely no question, the facts are there for all to see, that pipelines pose much less risk to the environment and to humans than trucks or trains.

By tapping into the tremendous wealth just beneath their feet, Quebec would not only become a much richer society but a much safer one as well!

CHAPTER FORTY-TWO

THE NATIVE INDIAN PROBLEM

In my book "Death in October", I write a final chapter that paints a very grim picture of life in Quebec after separation. Along with tremendous financial difficulties, in the book, the "Cree Nation" of northern Quebec has declared war on the Republic of Quebec, bringing the fledging republic to it knees by destroying power lines from the giant James Bay hydro project.

The book, of course is fiction. But more than that, that final chapter was written before I was aware of the vast reservoirs of oil and gas that would undoubtedly have to be tapped into by any new government of an independent Quebec. Forty six billion barrels of oil, trillions of cubic feet of natural gas, much of it relatively easily recoverable, and close to the vast eastern American seaboard market would create tremendous wealth, certainly more than enough to replace any transfers from the federal government.

The potential is there for the average Quebecers to find themselves a lot richer than they are today. In fact there may very well be more than a few of us in the rest of Canada kicking ourselves for letting Quebec and all that oil and gas money slip through our fingers!

But an independent Quebec would still face a serious problem. Native Indians, especially the Crees of northern Quebec.

As many of you know, just prior to the 1995 Quebec referendum vote, I received a phone call from Billy Diamond, the former Grand Chief of the Crees and a highly regarded and much revered figure within the Cree Nation. " Let your listeners and your friends in high places up there in Ottawa know that the Cree will fight," he whispered into the phone. "The Cree will fight!"

He was making it very plain—as have other Native Indian leaders—that their treaties are all with Canada and they will not allow themselves to lose that citizenship. I believe to this day that Billy's threat was a very real one, and had Quebecers at the time voted to succeed, violence might very well have ensued.

But that was then. This is now.

Today, there are three things that would almost certainly solve the problem

Let me suggest the following:

Number one—money—bags full of it solves a lot of problems. Indian chiefs today are not about to sell Manhattan or anything else for a few beads and mirrors. With billions pouring in from oil and gas royalties and taxes there will be more than enough money to smooth a lot of waters.

Number two—Native Indians are clamoring for more autonomy. Give it to them. They want some form of self-government. Give it to them.

Number three—Allow Native Indians to remain Canadian citizens. We have several million people scattered around the world who hold Canadian passports while living elsewhere, why would we deny Canadian citizenship to people born in this country who wish to remain citizens?

There is absolutely no way that Canada could withhold Canadian citizenship from any resident of an independent Quebec.

It would, of course, be up to the Republic of Quebec whether to grant dual citizenships. In other words, be a citizen of Quebec and of Canada, but at least when it comes to Native Indians, Quebec would not dare to deny them the right to continue to hold Canadian passports—keeping in mind of course, that as Canadian citizens, responsibility for much of their well-being would rest with Canada and not Quebec!

To sum up—provide Native Indians in the new Republic of Quebec a few truckloads of money, allow some form of negotiated self-government and allow them to remain as Canadian citizens. Problem solved? I suspect so!

The only problem actually might be with public opinion in the rest of Canada.

As you will see here, when I put the question to listeners on my show the reaction concerning dual citizenship was mixed.

The following is a sampling of emails I received from those who agreed that their full names be published.

CHAPTER FORTY-THREE

THE VOTERS SAY

Heard your show today, asking the question: When Quebec leaves should we grant them dual citizenship?

My answer is yes, as long as it doesn't benefit them economically. Let me explain; dual citizenship would give you cross border privileges, but not to go back and forth daily working at your job (i.e., Federal Government employees). You use our hospitals, you pay just as an American coming here would.

Putting strict limitations on dual citizenship would cut out all the abusers and users. It would also separate the real radical separatists from those who like and appreciate Canada and still be tourist friendly. Yes...I think it could work.

Hugh J. Grant, Green Valley, ON

~ • ~

No dual citizenship for Quebec
Terry Tysick, West Carleton, ON

~ • ~

As I have heard you say many times, we have granted dual citizenship to thousands if not millions of people who have never contributed anything to this country and never will. Therefore it would not be fair to deny Canadian citizenship to loyal Canadians who wish to remain Canadian but are living in an independent Quebec. To deny Canadian citizenship, for example, to Native Indians who have consistently made it clear they wish to remain Canadian would be completely unfair.

And I ask you this. How in the world could we deny Canadian citizenship to a Quebec resident who had fought for this country? No doubt some will take advantage of anything, but those who were born Canadian and wish to remain so should not be denied that right. And it would be a right.

Jane Twinning, Ottawa, ON

~ • ~

I disagree with dual citizenship. You are Canadian and you fall under our regulations. If you decided to go south for the winter you are obliged to cover your own expenses, so therefore if you take up residence in another country permanently you lose your citizenship. You should choose one or the other.

Kay Matthews, Ottawa, ON

~ • ~

You ask the question regarding possible dual citizenship for some people after Quebec separates. I don't have a big problem with the idea, except for, like all things, the prospect of abuse.

There are probably many people who sincerely want to remain closely connected to Canada, but I can see thousand of separatists getting dual citizenships, strictly to keep their cushy public service jobs in Ottawa.

Elizabeth Charland, North Gower, ON

~ • ~

Obviously the Cree would want to keep their land along with their citizenship and I think that would be very difficult to negotiate with Quebec. Achieving that would require that we work out the practical issues of Canada having access to the Cree and their territory.

The Cree desire to remain part of Canada seems to be at odds with many other Aboriginal groups that do not recognize Canada and its laws. I don't know what the Cree history is with these issues, but in principle I do not have any problem with them remaining Canadian.

Allowing the Cree to choose their own destiny then begs the question will Anglophones be offered the same right to choose? After all, Anglophone rights have been under attack for many years in Quebec and this will only increase with Quebec separation. If Anglophones can choose to retain their Canadian citizenship, how do we then afford them the "protection" of Canada since there isn't a recognized block of land belonging to the Anglophones? When you think about it, thus far Canada has done absolutely nothing to protect the English-speaking people in Quebec. Would there be a political will to do so within a separate Quebec?

The question about the Cree and Anglophone right to choose their country leads me to realize that we have been approaching this separation issue from the wrong perspective all along. We have assumed separation is for Quebec to decide and with that assumption we handed them the right to decide the future of Canada and all other provinces and territories. In other words, even on the topic of separation, we have been allowing the tail to wag the dog.

Your idea that it is Canada's decision to make if Quebec separates, not just Quebec's is a step in the right direction. For the first time there is recognition that Canada, as a whole, has the absolute right to decide its own future, not just one unhappy province. However, this is a complex question that cannot simply ask if we want Quebec to separate.

Several other questions have to be posed at the same time. For example, if you vote for Quebec separation, do you want Canada to cease being designated a bilingual country? This question is as important as the first because I would not trust any government to negotiate separation *unless we provide clear direction that we are not interested in maintaining the status quo.*

Habits are very hard to break and the long-standing habit of politicians in Canada has been to give in to Quebec at every turn.

We therefore need firm, straightforward negotiation orders, which for me would be: In a new Canada without Quebec, I do not want official bilingualism. I do not want jobs designated bilingual. I do not want promotions based on your ability to speak French. Bilingual services can still be provided where numbers warrant, but public sector workers should not be able to work in the language of their choice. The working language should be English and the public offered bilingual services where numbers warrant.

In other words, true practical bilingualism. I do not want health centers and community centers designated Francophone. I want everyone to be free to use any facility.

If the issue of bilingualism is not addressed and corrected as part of separation, we may as well keep Quebec. Otherwise, an even smaller percentage of our population will continue to have greater sway over our daily lives and that is not acceptable.

Sharon Navin, Nepean, ON

~ • ~

Dual citizenship. An interesting concept. We allow it for thousands of others around the world, so we would be hard pressed to deny Canadian citizenship to Quebec residents who wish to remain Canadian. I am especially concerned with the plight of Aboriginals who have made it very clear in the past that they have no truck or trade with a separate Quebec. Granting them the right to remain as Canadian citizens would be the fair and proper thing to do. As for everyone else in Quebec? Not so sure. Perhaps with some very strict provisions. For sure it will be over my dead body that Quebec residents be allowed to work for the Canadian government. No way Jose!

Marion, Scott, Oakville, ON

~ • ~

The major problem I see with granting dual citizenship to anyone, including residents of a newly formed Republic of Quebec is the right to employment. Especially employment with the Federal Government. With some reservations I would not be opposed to allowing those who wish to remain Canadian citizens a Canadian passport while living in Quebec, but I would strenuously deny the right of anyone living outside Canada to work for the Canadian government. We don't allow Americans living outside Canada to work for the feds, why would be allow residents of the Quebec Republic to do so?

Gerald Quick, Cornwall, ON

~ • ~

I just read that there could be as many as 350,000 residents of Hong Kong who have somehow been able to acquire Canadian passports. I find this outrageous, but nonetheless, if we're going to give half the people in China Canadian citizenship, why not Aboriginals in any new country called Quebec. Oh by the way, if Quebec separates will they have to change the name of the Montreal hockey club?

Dennis Easterbrook, Orleans, ON

~ • ~

I do not agree that Quebecers should have dual citizenship when they leave. They do not want to be part of Canada, so they will have chosen to give up citizenship.

The rest of Canada has been giving massive transfer payments to Quebec, but they continue to demand more. In addition, there is discrimination in the province against Anglophones. If Quebecers are granted dual citizenship they would continue to hold government jobs, further disadvantaging Anglophones.

We refuse to go to Quebec today because we just don't feel welcome there.

Frank Howey, Ottawa, ON

~ • ~

I cannot conceive of my Canada without Quebec, but if at some point, for whatever reason, the province does go its separate way, then yes anyone there who wishes should be able to retain his or her Canadian citizenship. This, among other things, would certainly separate the wheat from the chaff. It would be fun to watch the rabid separatists have to decide whether to retain citizenship in the Canada they tried to destroy or lose their job.

All those federal government employees in Gatineau, for example who have voted for separatists parties would be confronted with the fact that they would have to retain their Canadian citizenship in order to keep their jobs. That's if we decide to allow Quebec residents to continue working for a foreign government!

Anne Stephenson, Cornwall, ON

~ • ~

Holy cow bud! For sure, for sure we would okay our Indian friends to stay Canadian. Just try to stop them I should think. Maybe with Quebec a separate nation, we could persuade the Crees up there in the wild, wild north to ship you poor beggars in Ontario some of our cheap hydro power. What say you?

Rheal Seguin, Gatineau, QC

~ • ~

Here's what I say. We're going to give Algonquin Indians here in Ontario a good solid chunk of our province because somebody back maybe three hundred years or so ago did some hunting and trapping along the Ottawa River. Why not offer Quebec natives all the free land and lakes they want as well. What the hell, from what I see the Ontario government is desperate to give the province away so why draw the line at Ontario Indians. Let's face it. When the white man arrived here Indians were wandering all over the place chasing beaver, moose and what not. I'm pretty sure they made it across the river to the Quebec side, so let's give them whatever they want on both sides. It's the Canadian way. Correction. It's the Ontario way!

Ian Turnbull, Barrie, ON

~ • ~

CHAPTER FORTY-FOUR

WHAT HAPPENS TO ATLANTIC CANADA?

Interestingly enough, of all the hundreds of emails and phone calls I received concerning the fate of Quebec, only one dealt with the issue of Atlantic Canada. Which is not to say that it is of little or no concern to Canadians.

I recall during the months leading up to the 1995 referendum, many callers were more concerned about what would happen to the Maritime Provinces then they were about Quebec itself.

There was no real consensus; some expressed the fear that once Quebec was gone, the Atlantic Provinces would become so isolated they would surely join the United States. Others speculated that an independent Quebec would either cut off trade routes from the ROC to the east coast entirely, or impose sufficient tolls on roads, rails and the St. Lawrence Seaway to greatly restrict the passage of various goods.

Michael C who asked that I identify him only as living in Atlantic Canada, in his correspondence with me (Chapter three) presents one of the grimmest portraits of Quebec independence I've ever seen. He predicts that not only would Atlantic Canada join with the northeastern United States, but also since power in the ROC would shift westward,

Ontario would become resentful and separate, thus essentially destroying the entire country.

Says Michael, "Canada will disappear."

That view or anything close to it is total nonsense.

If anything, the ROC would be more united and homogeneous with the most disruptive ingredient in the country gone. Let's be very honest here. The only other province where any kind of serious separatist movement has even been kicked around by a bunch of the boys over a few beers is Alberta. And what has always struck in the craw of many Albertans? Come on, we all know the answer to that. What bothers Albertans most is Quebec and its special privileges and the billions of dollars it sucks out of Albertan pockets without so much as a thank you.

What isn't generally known, or has been forgotten, is that in 1981 right, after Pierre Trudeau's disastrous National Energy Programme which collapsed Alberta's oil boom, a poll indicated that 49 per cent of Alberta voters supported separation from Canada. Alberta cars began sporting bumper stickers saying, "Let the Eastern Bastards Freeze in the Dark!" Remembers those days?

In retaliation against Trudeau's imposition of the NEP, Alberta Premier Peter Lougheed cut the flow of western oil to the east by five per cent in March of 1981, then a few months later increased the cut to ten per cent.

Those were not happy days in Canada, but despite the tremendous animosity in the West towards Ontario and Quebec, there was never any serious attempt at separation.

Nonetheless, anyone who thinks Alberta today would grieve the loss of Quebec isn't paying attention or has suddenly arrived here from another planet!

As for any of the Atlantic Provinces leaving Canada and joining the United States—it will never happen! Maritimers have always been proud and loyal Canadians and always will be. Actually it's insulting to residents there to suggest they could easily switch allegiances from their country to another.

And as for the Atlantic Provinces being geographically cut of. Let's think about that. Cut off how? Quebec, as an independent country, will still be there. So will all the roads, the railways and the St. Lawrence Seaway. Good heavens, we ship about 80 per cent of everything we manufacture and grow in Canada down to the United States, using their roads, their railways, pipelines, waterways, etc. Why would it be any different in Quebec? Does anything really think that just because its political status has changed the province (or the new country) will suddenly impede or halt commerce?

The drive, flight or rail time from Toronto to Halifax will remain as it is today. There need not even be a border stop. You can drive or take a train or boat all the way from Greece to Ireland today and never once be stopped at a border. You don't even need a passport for goodness sake. If Europe, only a few years after dropping bombs on each other can get along this well why couldn't we? Of course we could and will.

And think of this. When Quebec is forced to stop being our leading welfare state and begins pumping oil and gas out of the ground, much of it will, in all probability, have to be shipped to worldwide markets from east coast ports. The largest refinery today in eastern Canada is in St. John, New Brunswick.

Quebec separation and the exploitation of their vast natural resources would create an economic boom for the Atlantic Provinces.

And as for Maritimers feeling so psychologically removed from Canadian life that they join the United States, let me ask you this. Have you ever visited Alaska? Because if you have, what you will find are the most fiercely proud, loyal and patriotic Americans in all 50 states. Many Alaskans will tell you that it is precisely because they are so geographically removed from the rest of their country that the isolation has actually enhanced their patriotism.

Visit Hawaii today and I swear you are going to see more Stars and Stripes flying from office buildings and homes than you ever see our flag in this country, even on Canada Day. That's one mighty long haul from California to Hawaii, no matter how you travel but ask any Hawaiian and they'll assure you they feel just as American as anyone in the mainland!

The last time I checked the shortest ferryboat ride from mainland Canada to Newfoundland is about eight hours. Heck, you can fly to Vancouver in less time than that, but the many miles of cold Atlantic water that separate the "Rock" from the rest of the country in no way makes Newfoundlanders feel less Canadian. Correct me if I am wrong, but didn't Newfoundlanders vote to join Canada a few years ago?

When you think about it, it makes sense. You will never feel more Canadian than when a group of you gets together in a foreign country. The Canadian Men's and Women's Club of the Bahamas launches every meeting with a rousing version of "Oh Canada". It sends chills up your spine!

And think of this, there are few people in the world who take more pride in their citizenship than Bahamians—who occupy more than 700 islands strung out along the ocean for more than 500 miles! There was much anguish and soul searching following the last federal election in the Bahamas because of the fact that voter turnout had dropped from the 2007 election. Editorials in Bahamian newspapers raged at the population for their lack of interest and patriotism.

It really wasn't much of a drop however—only down to 90.78 per cent in 2012 from 92.13 per cent in 2007! The distance between islands doesn't seem to have deterred Bahamian national identity or pride very much does it?

Nationality, loyalty, love and pride of country are states of mind, not a state of geography!

Quebec will eventually separate because it is already a separate place, distinct from the rest of Canada. Its residents, for the most part, have very little in common with those in other provinces. The average Quebecois would find life as strange in Brantford, Ontario as he or she would in Athens, Greece. Both places would be foreign territory, just as increasingly Quebec City or any place in Quebec has become foreign territory for most of those living in the ROC.

Let's be very honest here. Most Albertans would probably feel more at home in Florida than in Quebec. Come to think of it, I suspect most Quebecers feel more at home in Florida than they would in Alberta!

The rest of the country, I am certain, will breathe a sign of relief, perhaps shed a little tear for a lost and noble dream when Quebec declares independence, but then we'll all get on with the business of creating a, richer, happier and far more unified country.

The most thorough examination of the consequences of Quebec independence is contained in a book entitled, "The Secession of Quebec and the Future of Canada" by Robert A. Young. Co-published by the Institute of Intergovernmental Relations at Queen's University, research for the study was undertaken partly though the auspices of the Institute and concludes among other things that, "Quebec could be excised from the existing Canadian Constitution very neatly!"

In other words, since Quebec has not signed our Constitution, removal of the province from Confederation would not pose a serious legal problem.

The study also made some very interesting observations concerning some of the logistics of Quebec separation. For example while separation would mean Canada losing about 6.9 million people the ROC would still be left with 74.7 per cent of the population and retain 84.5 per cent of its present territory.

Furthermore, the study found the ROC today attracts about 80 percent of all private investment and by far the largest share of immigration, factors unlikely to change with the absence of Quebec.

And here's an interesting finding. With the absence of Quebec, French as mother tongue in the ROC would be outnumbered three to one by those whose mother tongue is neither French nor English. The language spoken in the homes of those living in the ROC would be 88 per cent English. Ontario would have 49 per cent of the ROC's population.

The study is extremely detailed and scholarly and deals with the Canadian experience before and after the 1995 Quebec referendum.

Among its conclusions is that Quebec separation is certainly within the realm of possibility and would not prove devastating to the economies of either Quebec or the ROC.

It's worthwhile noting here that these findings were arrived at before the discovery of vast amounts of oil and gas beneath the surface of Quebec. How that discovery would change the findings of the study is impossible to say. One would think, however, that a much richer Quebec than first believed would not be a deterrent to separation nor impede the economic development of Quebec or the ROC.

The study finds that there are several different Constitutional paths we could follow after Quebec is gone, but the most likely scenario would be that our Constitution and form of government would retain the status quo. The entire study is available through Queen's University.

CHAPTER FORTY-FIVE

WE'RE BANKERS TO THE SEPARATISTS!

I know that compared to all other costs involved in trying to keep this country together it's not a lot of money but I have to ask the question anyway since I suspect it's an issue that disturbs many of us. As we saw with the infamous $16 glass of orange juice, the $90 thousand Mike Duffy cheque, sometimes it's the little things that really drive you crazy. So here's the question:

How do you like the fact that so far we have poured more than half a billion dollars into the pockets and purses of separatist members of parliament? Adding insult to injury we're pouring millions more into their bank accounts every year and will continue to do so as long as you're alive.

Let me explain:

According to a study by the CBC every backbench federal Member of Parliament costs us taxpayers $590,668.90 a year

That figure, says the CBC, is a sum of MP's salary, pension and other expenditures.

Here's a brief summary of those yearly costs as reported by the CBC.

Salary—$157,731 (actually increased to about $160,000 in 2013).

Office Budget—$284,700. This includes employees salaries, service contracts, constituency office leases, office operating expenses and travel, including employee travel.

Accommodation and per diem expenses—$25,850. This includes expenses incurred while traveling on parliamentary business and those related to maintaining a secondary residence in Ottawa. These expenses do not include flight and other transportation costs which come out of the MPs office and House of Commons budgets. Every MP is allocated 64 travel points each fiscal year with one point equal to one return trip.

House of Commons costs—$118,098,64 (but highly variable by MP). This is the cost of the goods and services provided by the House of Commons to an MP in the course of helping them do their job. This includes everything from printing to phone service as well as furniture and some travel expenses for the MP and staff members.

Pension—$54,693 per year (current MP who serves until 2015 or $64,985 (current MP who serves until 2019)

Election Expenses—$383,333.33 per MP per election

This figure is based on government estimates that it will cost an additional $11.4 million per election to pay for 30 new MPs who will be elected to parliament during the next election.

Other Budgets—Cabinet ministers, and other MPs, including some opposition MPs receive additional salaries and benefits depending upon the roles they assume.

So you ask how did you arrive at the figure of more than half a billion dollars to pay for separatist MPs since they were first elected in 1993?

You do the math.

In 1993 the Bloc Quebecois elected 54 members—at roughly $590,000 per year that's about $32 million per year—four years—$128 million.

(By the way from 1993 until the election in 1997 the Bloc was Canada's official opposition party which meant, among other things, that many of its members received salaries and benefits well above the CBC figure of $590,668.90!)

In 1997 the Bloc elected 44 members—cost about $26 million per year—four years—$104 million

In 2000 the Bloc elected 38 members—cost about $22 million per year—four years——$88 million

In 2004 the Bloc elected 54 members—cost about $32 million per year—two years——$64 million.

In 2006 the Bloc elected 51 members—cost about $30 million per year—two years——$60 million

In 2008 the Bloc elected 49 members—cost about $29 million per year—four years——-$116 million

In 2011 the Bloc elected four members—cost about $2 million per year—approximately two years—$4 million. (In 2013 an NDPer defected to the Bloc, bringing the Bloc total to five, then in September of 2013, a Bloc MP rebelled against the Quebec Charter of Values and left the Party bringing their number down to four again!)

Total cost to Canadian taxpayers from 1993 until today for separatist MP salaries, benefits, office costs and pensions—About $564 million—well over half a billion dollars and millions more each year in pensions alone!

Admittedly, these are approximate figures, but if you believe the findings of the CBC, they give us a fairly accurate picture of what it costs Canadian taxpayers to support Quebec MPs who do not have the best interests of our country at heart.

With only four members in the House now, obviously the separatists don't have their hands into our bank accounts as deeply as in the past, but let's not forget the fact that even though the Harper Government has reduced MP's pensions considerably, we're still forking over millions every year in pensions for people whose stated goal was to break the country apart! Former Bloc leader Gilles Duceppe, for example, will receive a nice little pay cheque from us of $120,392 every year for the rest of his life! Nice work if you can get it eh?

It is true, of course, that the cost of keeping MPs in office is the same whether they are separatists or not. If Liberals or Conservatives or even the NDP had occupied those seats rather than the separatists the cost would have been about the same.

The difference of course would be that taxpayers from coast to coast would not be forced to bankroll MPs who freely admit they have no interest in the welfare of Canada and Canadians outside Quebec. I can find no other country in the world where federal taxpayers are forced to pay the salaries, benefits and pensions of those whose stated goal is the break-up of the country.

So long as Quebec remains part of Canada this folly will continue.

And of course there is this.

Quebec has 75 federal seats (3 more in the next election) at $590,668.90 per year—that's an annual cost of more than $44 million to pay for MPs of all political stripes in that province, many of them with little or no interest in the betterment of Canada as a whole. Couple that with all the other costs associated with keeping Quebec within Confederation and you really have to ask yourself these questions.

Are we getting our money's worth?

Has the price of keeping Quebec in Canada become too high?

As with the Czech Republic and Slovakia, would we be better friends after a "velvet divorce"?

What is it we are afraid of?

CHAPTER FORTY-SIX

TOMORROW

I have no illusions concerning the ingredients this book will toss into to the ever-roiling stewpot of opinion that is constantly on the boil concerning Quebec's role within Canada. No one is going to flip the final page, hurl the book through the kitchen window, rush to Parliament Hill and join angry multitudes demanding that Quebec immediately absent itself from Canada.

That's not the way things work in Canada, nor should it be.

Any decision involving the fate of a country deserves a very thorough, very sober national debate.

National means that all of Canada must not only take part in this debate, but will insist that any decision concerning Quebec separation will not be just a regional one but national.

But the debate must be an honest and open one where people feel free to express their true feelings without fear of being labeled a racist or worse.

An understanding of some of the facts I have presented here can only assist in such a debate. I do not believe, for example, that most

Canadians are aware of the tremendous wealth of oil and gas that sits just beneath the surface of Quebec soil. For generations we have been confronted with the argument on both sides that separation would be a financial disaster for Quebec. Very clearly this is not the case and I think I have made that point very graphically.

This fact alone changes the debate dramatically!

One of the things I hope this book accomplishes is to remind people that the rest of Canada (the ROC) has just as much right to hold referendums on whether to expel Quebec as Quebec has to decide to leave. For far too long the orthodoxy has been that that decision is Quebec's alone.

Wrong!

In fact, when you read this book you will be hard pressed not to conclude that if anyone has reason to demand a divorce it is the ROC. Tally up the list of legitimate grievances over the years and it's like comparing the Carp Creek with the Fraser River. (Three guesses whose list is the Fraser?)

While I know what I have to say here will anger and disappoint some people, including some members of my family, I firmly believe that I am only placing on the record what the overwhelming majority of Canadians outside Quebec have been feeling, thinking in some cases saying for some time. And, I might add, more than a few residents of Quebec as well!

At the very least it is my hope that this book will prompt a sufficient outcry across the ROC to either halt or drastically reduce transfer payments being plowed into Quebec. This decision must be made before the end of 2014 by the Harper Government and is bound to have widespread ramifications no matter what the final outcome.

If the transfer payments are stopped to Quebec, as they should be, or greatly reduced, there is no doubt in my mind that it will very quickly prompt another referendum on separation which will most likely be won by the separatists. We must be prepared for this.

On the other hand if the government continues to pour billions more into a province that very clearly has the ability to create enormous wealth on its own, I think a separation movement will be launched within the ROC which, unless I am reading the situation entirely incorrectly, could very well lead to Canada waving a friendly good bye to Quebec.

I would far sooner this decision be made by the people of Quebec so I say to them, rather than kicking around your minorities in an effort to preserve your language and culture, why not do what many other countries have done.

Be brave, be bold, cut the ties, become an independent country. Become "masters in your own house". The mood is such in the rest of Canada today that there will be no hard feelings. We'll be fair in dividing up the spoils. Heaven only knows we've always bent over backwards to accommodate and be fair to Francophones no matter where they live.

Quebecers, demonstrate to the world that you care as much about your language and culture as Irishmen did when they stood up to everything Britain could hurl at them and formed their own republic. Believe me when I say Canada won't throw anything at you, except probably good wishes.

The world is filled with nations that overcame tremendous obstacles; sometimes shed blood in order to achieve independence, starting of course with the neighbour just to your south.

You can do it Quebec. Get yourself off the welfare roles. Get some pride in yourselves. Get your politicians' noses out of the trough. Tap into the black gold that lies beneath your feet. What are you waiting for?

Your ancestors were the toughest people in the world. They were afraid of nothing the land and its hostile forces could hurl at them.

What is it you are afraid of? A few Anglos? Cutting the apron strings?

Toughen up Quebec! Do it. It will be a very amicable divorce.

A velvet divorce. But don't make us in the ROC do it. You do it and we'll have a little party.

Hell, make it a big party!

Then let's all be friends. Better friends!

I have included the comments and stories of some 90 Canadians in this book. In fact the more than 300 emails and other correspondence I have received to date would fill many more chapters. The issue of national unity is obviously of great concern to most Canadians and rightly so. If you have any further thoughts about Quebec's role in the Canada of tomorrow or about anything you have read here, please contact me at lgreen@cfra.com.

Very clearly this issue is far from over!

Lowell Green